# QUAINT SCOTS

## of Bygone Days

# QUAINT SCOTS
## of Bygone Days

BY

D. C. CUTHBERTSON

ENEAS MACKAY
STIRLING

FIRST PUBLISHED   -   1939

PRINTED AT
THE OBSERVER PRESS, STIRLING, SCOTLAND

# CONTENTS

# ILLUSTRATIONS

del
ha
is
wc
ou

# FOREWORD

In the following chapters I have endeavoured to ineate some of the bygone Scots whose lives and deeds ve appealed to me. Whether it is because our country small and our population sparse, and that men and men of strong character and outstanding ability stand it more prominently by virtue of the fact, I cannot hazard an opinion, but it appears to me that this old land of ours has produced its share of notabilities.

To-day, perhaps, we live too close to our environment to see our contemporaries in their due proportion. It may be that stress of modern conditions, development of industrial cities and centres, makes us run to type; whatever the reason, we become more uniform, more reflective of " mass production " in our actions and reactions to life in general than was the case a century or two ago. Industry has commanded the best of our creative power, and in a material sense that is all to the good; but life lacks the colour it had a few generations ago, the leisurely gait has been speeded to a feverish rush, the journey has become irksome in the desire to arrive. That is the reason why I sometimes think it is good to pause and look back on these quaint, outstanding characters whose names still live, it may be only as names preserved in dusty archives, but nevertheless preserved for those who wish to study and observe.

With a few exceptions, those whom I have dealt with, in mere outline it is true, were men and women of the eighteenth century, a time when Scotland was

developing rapidly under the Union. It was an unco
period socially but definitely a century of progress. W
the final result of the '45, feudal and baronial rights w
being commuted by the Government at a cost of hundr
of thousands of pounds and men could sleep safely
night, the memories of Claverhouse and his Dragoo.
the risk of a Highland Host, banished in a more peace.
atmosphere.

And now the reader must be the judge, but I shou
like to take this opportunity of acknowledging my indebte
ness to the proprietors of " The Scottish Field " fo
permission to reproduce these essays, as all, with one
exception, the chapter on Lord Braxfield, appeared in that
journal. I should also like to pay tribute to Mr. R. J.
Prentice for permitting the reproduction of the illustrations
which give life to the pages and entailed such time and
research on his part to obtain.

D. C. C.

MARLIN LODGE,
    By NEWTON MEARNS.
        November, 1939.

# INTRODUCTION

THROUGH the long pages of Scotland's story marches a silent pageant of great men and women. Here and there in the vast procession we get a passing glimpse of an outstanding personality, remarkable even amongst the illustrious figures of bygone days. Not necessarily a statesman remembered even now for his foresight and vision; not a man of letters noted for his erudition, or a great divine revered for his life and work; not even a man of the sword whose deeds added a lustre to his country's fame. Those we shall meet may include humbler folk, upon whom the sun of public applause failed to shine during their living years, who reaped no harvests from the fields which they tilled, but whose names are still green, and who will be remembered when the more exalted are forgotten and their words and deeds become as the smoke of a fire that is spent.

Every really outstanding man or woman has added a tincture to the life of the community. No remarkable personality can tread the earthly stage without leaving some subtle essence which colours the lives of those who have looked on from stalls or gallery. When the final curtain has been rung down, and the applause or derision is silenced and forgotten, memories of words or actions linger on, embalmed in tradition and romance or preserved in dusty records.

A present-day South African writer, in a somewhat cynical passage, speaks about a discovery, or rather invention, as not of supreme importance, because it did not help to produce more food, or more noise, or a quicker or more wholesale instrument of slaughter, and so was not of any direct utility to human beings! The modern world may change and alter until national characteristics are merged into a vast cosmopolitanism, but always the truly great will stand high above their fellows, like beacons on the troubled sea of life. It will be a bad day for our own land when our great sons and daughters are doomed to obscurity and when frontiers of thought and character are swept away on the tide of commercial materialism.

Sometimes it is a little difficult, or at least obscure for us, to follow the lives of those who have long since passed away. The results are there all right for every man to note, but what Burns termed " the moving why they do it " is not just clear. I think it is because they were natural. Nothing false or artificial goes on living until it becomes, as our chosen examples have become, immortal figures—our country's history. Not really great figures, but still undying names.

Perhaps William Seabrook has the secret in a passage in his " White Monk of Timbuctoo." I think so ; but here it is :—" The choice . . . is not always easy, perhaps not always best, certainly not always profitable. To be a man or a Churchman. To be a man or a rich man. To be a man or a Governor. To be a man or a poet. To be a man or a great composer, virtuoso, or surgeon. A man or a corner grocery-man for that matter. A man or a best seller. A man or a copy-righted name on a brand of soap, a book, or an office. It is not easy to be both. It is not easy to choose. It is not very easy to think about."

The history of Scotland is a rather checkered page, and perhaps that accounts in part for the many odd and outstanding characters who from time to time have figured in her annals. A poor country always, barren and unproductive, not blessed with a very genial climate, independence and character in her sons alone saved the race. A few years ago a great divine, speaking at a dinner in London, said that the virtues of Scotsmen were due to three men and one woman. His selection was William Wallace, John Knox and Robert Burns, and Mary Queen of Scots, whom he could imagine saying after her recent meeting at Jedburgh with Sir James Barrie (referring to a then recent speech by the great playright)—" Whether my eyes are blue or hazel, they still do their old job of diddling sentimental Scotsmen!"

That may be true of the home-keeping Scot; but to my way of thinking the Scotland known to the outside world, with its real or imaginary glamour, is due in great measure to the deeds and words of three men, all of whom were born within the eighteenth century. The three are Bonnie Prince Charlie, Robert Burns, and Sir Walter Scott. Round each name has been woven a cloak of tradition and romance, until each figure has assumed a stature greater than that of many other outstanding personalities. They are really deified super-beings, lower than the gods but towering above other men no matter how gifted.

On the dark field of Drummossie Moor the spirit of chivalry was finally drowned in blood. But the deeds of the tartan-clad clansmen, their chiefs, above all the impetuous Charles Edward Stuart, gave birth to a very torrent of song and ballad, legend and romance, which is to-day a national heritage. The glamour of the Highlands is alive to-day because of that fact. What the '45 did for the Highlands, Robert Burns by other methods achieved for the south-west lowlands. He pictured everyday life as he knew it : the toil and poverty, the cheer and hypocrisy, the dour Covenanting temperament, and he worked in such a manner that the clay became gold in his hands. Scott took the old tales and traditions and wove them into imperishable words. But he did even more than that. He gave us a clean, healthy literature, free from the sordid and vulgar elements so common in his day. He set a standard too high for many of his brothers of the pen, but by that he ensured his position for all time.

Great as were these men, they did something more which holds our interest. They shed their light on lesser mortals and made these others also live for all time. People like the common run of most, who would have lived their short span and have been forgotten by all save their own immediate contemporaries.

But for the '45, the kilt might—I do not say would, but certainly might—have been as dead and forgotten, as a social garment, as are the breeches and shillelagh of the sister isle. The Lowland ladies wore the tartan in defiance when such adornment was proscribed by law. Captain Burt tells us that the lowlands were first in the use of tartan, and they got the fashion from France, as the word implies. The word " kilt " is essentially lowland in its derivation, and really means a short garment. To-day the dress at once places the wearer in the category of a Highlander, but a glance at any reference book or family history will show that most of the leading Lowland families had their distinguishing tartan.

Be that as it may, the Bonnie Prince Charlie episode brought upon our stage many actors otherwise unknown— Flora Macdonald, Lochiel, Cluny Macpherson, Lord George Murray, Lovat, Duncan Forbes, and Dr. Archibald Cameron, to take only a few and as they occur to mind. In November, 1925, the Archbishop of York dedicated the bells of Carlisle Cathedral ere they rang out a peal—the first for 180 years ! The earlier peal had welcomed the Highland army to the city on that ill-fated march South, and as a punishment a cowardly government forbade them to ring again. Right or wrong, these were men who played such parts—a handful against a nation.

The figures immortalised by Burns were perhaps more humble in station but no whit less interesting. Tam Samson's dead, as is his greater contemporary, Tam o' Shanter, but neither is likely to be forgotten. How many folks, I wonder, who have visited Tarbolton during the last fifty years for the one purpose of " todlin' doon on Willie's mill " have resisted the impulse to be seated for a moment on the stone by the braeside and to reflect on that scene when Death talked to Dr. Hornbook ?

As for Scott, his heroes, too, are part of our everyday knowledge, and, like the others, have passed the greatest test of all, in other words, are of familiar significance even to many who have not actually read about them. Jeanie Deans, Madge Wildfire, Lucy Ashton, Meg Merrilees, Dugald Dalgetty, Old Mortality, and we certainly cannot omit Rob Roy—these were all based on living characters, men and women who lived their short span, and who did not then disappear into the limbo of forgotten things only because a master hand had drawn them on the parchment of immortality. The Johnnie Armstrongs and Kinmont Willies of the Borders, the Rob Roys and Black Duncans of the Westlands, have no place in modern life, but they fitted into their own times, and our reading of a night at the fireside would be the poorer without them. But our figures were not all fighting men, reivers and outlaws, or devotees of that " convivial Caledonia " spirit which so intrigues and amuses the superior beings who really know nothing about our country and its people other than from a few alleged jokes or an occasional rather vulgar and wholly unrepresentative comedian.

Even our supposedly national beverage is an outsider, foisted on us in lieu of claret and small beer.    Whisky in its original form probably originated in China and travelled across Europe before finding a secure haven beside the peat-burns of the North.

Of course, few of our great Scots figure even in the long galleries of the three figures touched upon.    They were models, not sculptors.    Many who might be better known laboured on, unappreciated while alive : forgotten in death ; but now and then a name crops up because of some incident.    Small as is our land, we do not all see alike. Claverhouse, whose very name is still held in loathing amongst the Ayrshire hills and hamlets, was an idol in the North—Great John of the Battles.    Than John Knox and Claverhouse no two men ever differed more widely in outlook, temperament and principle ; and yet, by a strange turn of the wheel, each took a wife from under the same roof.    Minor history, the lives of men and women, is rich in such anomalies.    Our ballad tales, the stories told amidst the peat-reek of the *ceilidh*, all weave romance round lives that were lived in harsh and often cruel times. Then, as now, few men lived fat and did things that really mattered.

Even our streams and hills are alive to-day, instinct with a romance and entity of their own, because of their association with bygone days.    Yarrow, Ettrick, Tweed— these are names to awaken dreams and stir the imagination. The thought of St. Mary's Loch brings Hogg knocking at the portals of memory.    Doon, Afton and Nith are not mere running water, but living streams because of their associations. Ben Dorian takes the mind flying back to Duncan Ban MacIntyre—and before his days to the sad chapter of Glencoe. Balquhidder is alive in memory of Rob Roy. Wander amongst the lonely hill-paths on the uplands of Ayrshire, and the spirit of the Covenanters will join with you again. Turn your eyes towards Solwayside, and the dreaded figure of Grierson of Lag will leap to meet you from amongst the smoke of burning farm steadings. The pioneering spirit of adventure was a strong characteristic of our grandfathers' days, and even now a wandering Scot turns up in most out-of-the-way places. But travel of a hundred or two years ago and travel of to-day are vastly different things, although let it be said in justice that there are fewer worlds to conquer and nearly everything has been done once !

No stranger figure ever perambulated Europe and the wider realms than that of old Lithgow, and no stranger chapters were ever written than those of his " Rare Adventures." The account of his tortures in Spain almost makes one's flesh creep, yet he recounts them with a strange admixture of gusto and pride. Or again, that rare spirit of David Livingstone, a man of some generations later but a son of the same county, who carried a torch into darkest Africa and whose life and work are an example to most. Mungo Park and Bruce, and later Mary Slessor, are Scottish names we are proud to honour—and they do not stand alone where dark tracks are followed and unknown paths explored.

The name of Snell is one blessed by many a needy scholar ; McCrimmon and Niel Gow have added much to the pleasure of our lighter hours ; Governor Macrae has amused us with his cantrips ; and Boswell left behind a biography which the world accepts as a model. Black

B

Agnes of Dunbar, Tibbie Pagan, Catherine Douglas, Flora Macdonald—perhaps the reader will think them rather ill-assorted examples, but again they are noted as they come unbidden to mind. Our pageant is composed of such—they bore no sceptres and wore no crowns, but each of them has left behind an interesting individual record, and out of forgotten millions that means something worth investigating.

Scotland is steeped in traditional tales assembled round the figures who forged her history in the centuries that are gone. Ruthless men of the sword, adventurers and pioneers—strange people to study and ponder over. Austere, devout ministers who would die for their faith and yet callously condemn poor, demented old women to the stake as witches. Fair, gentle ladies who crowded light-heartedly to public executions in the spirit in which to-day's society attends the opera. Honest, kind-hearted folks whose chief diversion was cock-fighting or badger-drawing—men complex, uncouth, but unwavering in their ideals, building the fabric of our history as we to-day know it. Back to the pageant, then, that we may have a nearer view of some members of that notable procession as it passes in silent order through the annals of our homeland.

# DUNCAN BAN MacINTYRE

## The Westland Poet

THE proverbial saying, " It's a far cry to Lochow," has lost its force to-day. Now, when you leave Dalmally for Loch Awe and Inveraray, it is by means of a broad, new highway. Your way lies closer to the loch than of yore, and Kilchurn is almost by the roadside. No view in all the beautiful westland—in Scotland itself, for that matter—surpasses that of Kilchurn with the loch spreading away in the distance and Ben Cruachan towering stark from the shore, especially when a white mutch of autumn snow adds to the grandeur of it all.

There is more traffic nowadays than was the case even a few years ago, and sometimes I think Cruachan looks down upon the modern world with a forgivable cloud upon his brow. Perhaps he has not quite forgotten the vandals who carried away the walls of Kilchurn to build, as some say, an inn ; others claim a more stately house in a neighbouring shire. Be that as it may, there are walls enough left to make Sir Colin Campbell's fifteenth century stronghold the most picturesque ruin in our land, apt and fitting for its unexcelled setting.

If the new highway echoes with noisy exhausts, there is compensation in the quietude of the old winding road, with its twists and turns, its neglected surface given over to hikers and others who prefer to tramp quietly amidst the beauty, even if passing years—or the miles behind— demand an occasional halt on the short steep ascents. It is a panorama of charming vistas ; stretching moorland, towering hills, the great expanse of Loch Awe, patches of woodland ; and far behind, on the road one has travelled, Ben More seems to peer wistfully across the intervening heights, as if loath to part with an old friend.

As you tramp along you will think to yourself ; what a land to enrapture a poet and to invite his praise ! And then you will come upon a strange little monument, dominant upon a hill top. The hill is Creagan-Chaorach—the Craig of the Sheep, and the monument is erected in memory of a poet, Duncan Ban MacIntyre—Fair Duncan of the Songs.

Not that Duncan was alone in his singing. Ian Lom, another old poet, and Duncan MacIntyre were both born in the same glen, whence, too, came the forbears of John Ruskin—no mean tribute to the world. Over the hills, a short mile or two, and itself on a hill, stands the monument to Neil Munro, another great soul. Behind, amidst the glens of Balquhidder, was born Dougal Buchanan. All these were men of the hills and glens, articulate with the beauties of their land.

Sometimes, when I climb the Craig of the Sheep and pause for a little to drink in the beauties spread on every hand, the only sound that of the motors on the new road—for sound carries far in such a spot—with never a human being in sight, I draw a mental picture. Foolish, I know, but it comes unbidden and will not depart. Somehow, in my mind it is associated with the place. The picture is of a world that is too busy to-day on the arterial road of life to loiter in the quiet byways with the old poets and singers. The moss and heather of neglect are gradually encroaching, and what was once considered a wide roadway will constrict to a hill-path, and gradually shrink and disappear.

Even so ; but it will not be quite deserted. Always

there will pass a strange shade, highland in garb; an old bonnet pulled well down over a high, thoughtful brow, a bonnet decked with the tail of a badger or some wild denizen of the hills; an old-time soldier's pack strapped on his shoulders. He will be armed, too, because he lived in troublous times—a period of which someone has said " the noble freebooter was being degraded into a common thief." Cattle lifting was ceasing to be a ploy, and the arm of the law was becoming longer.

But this figure was no reiving freebooter. Donacha Ban loved that countryside too well not to haunt it in the minds of those who dwell on such things and who love to ponder on the old days and on the quaint figures, greater than their neighbours realised, who sang and toiled and battled ere entering into the shadow land and becoming a memory.

It has been said more than once, but it will bear repetition, that what Robert Burns was to lowland Scotland, so was Duncan MacIntyre to the Gaelic-speaking western highlands. Like Burns, he was a son of the soil, born in even more humble circumstances, his whole life a struggle against fate, his only weapons his own undaunted spirit.

When it is realised that this poet, whose words are in the mouths and hearts of thousands of highland folk to-day, whose songs awaken memories in many a lonely outpost overseas, could neither read nor write, one realises also the virile type of man he must have been, and how futile is our civilisation that could allow such genius to pass virtually unnoticed. Perhaps, however, this neglect was not such a tragedy. Education and polish might have spoilt Duncan's simple outlook and dried up his natural spring—I do not know.

To Dr. Stewart of Luss, whose father was minister of

the neighbouring parish, and who became interested in the poet, we owe a debt of gratitude. At that time MacIntyre was, I think, employed as gamekeeper on a nearby estate, and realising the worth and beauty of his verse, Dr. Stewart made him recite his compositions and carefully preserved and prepared them for publication. The poet was then nearing middle age, about his forty-fourth year, yet so retentive was his memory that he could repeat songs and verses without halt or confusion. Dr. Stewart took down some six thousand lines of verse from oral dictation.

If the lives of Burns and Duncan MacIntyre were parallel in their untutored genius and material poverty, the mental outlook of the two poets is altogether dissimilar. At times Burns was soured and embittered by his lot, and this discontent occasionally coloured his outlook and judgment. Not so Fair-haired Duncan. Spontaneous and free, his songs were always sweet and kindly—there was not a doubtful thought in his mind. Indeed, simplicity of outlook and a single-minded pleasure in the day's task were the basic notes of his whole career. His wife Mairi : the hills and glens of his native land : the beasts and birds and streams—these were the themes that inspired his delicate, clean and kindly muse.

To know the real beauty of the Gaelic speech, one must be familiar with the tongue, and if this is so with prose, how much more so must it be with verse ? That is perhaps the reason why Duncan MacIntyre is not known and appreciated so widely as he merits.

One of his best pieces is named " Coire Cheathoich," or "The Misty Corri." It is too long to reproduce here, but it opens with a picture of the Corri, and then—so keen is his observation, so wide his loving knowledge—he mentions almost every flower and plant on the hillside,

from "the twisted hemlock" to the "close-set groundsel."
He goes on to tell us that :

> In every nook of the mountain pathway
>   The garlic-flower may be thickly found—
> And out on the sunny slopes around it
>   Hang berries juicy and red and round—
> The penny-royal and dandelion,
>   The downy cannoch together lie—
> Thickly they grow from the base of the mountain
>   To the topmost crag of his crest so high.

He does not forget the daisies, primroses, sorrel, while :

> " . . . not a crag but is clad most richly,
>   For rich and silvern the soft moss clings.
> Fine is the moss, most clean and stainless,
>   Hiding the look of unlovely things."

The salmon leaping and the " dun-brown deer " are
commented upon, and then the bird life of the hill comes
within the poet's keen vision.    " The red cock murmuring
close at hand.    While the little wren blew his tiny trumpet,"
the speckled thrush and the redbreast are amongst those
where :

> " Not a singer but joined in the chorus,
>   Not a bird in the leaves was still :
>
>   .    .    .    .    .    .
>
> Everywhere  was  the  blithesome  chorus,
>   Till the glen was murmuring thro' and thro'."

Perhaps Duncan is at his height in the verses devoted
to the red-deer, but even then he finds time to note the
bees that fly humming amidst the flowers.   This poem of
the misty glen is the poet at his best, describing something
which he knew and loved as only a highlander loves his
native hills—and this was the land he had known and dwelt
in from birth to middle age.

It was his home-land because MacIntyre was born in a small cottage—a but-and-ben—on the hillside above Inveroran, on March 20, 1724. Even to-day, two-hundred years later, Druimliart or Drumlaighart of Glenorchy is a silent, lonely spot, and the ruined walls of the humble birth-place are fast crumbling to decay—they might long since have disappeared but for the fact that they are used at times for penning sheep. There is, I believe, a proposal to employ the stones as a cairn to mark the spot—a project certain to meet with favour in many quarters.

When a youth of twenty-one, and although against his natural inclinations, Duncan MacIntyre fought on the Government side in the '45. He acted as substitute for Fletcher of Glenorchy, the fee to be three hundred merks (Scots) and the sword the one which the inglorious laird should personally have wielded. At the Battle of Falkirk the Prince's Highlanders had a one-sided victory, and the poet ran with the lave, following the example of many panic-stricken red-coats, and throwing away his weapon.

When Duncan made his way home again and reported to Fletcher, that gentleman refused to pay the fee, on the ground that the sword was his property and had not been returned! The poet retorted with a satire of which Fletcher was the butt, and the affair coming to the notice of the Earl of Breadalbane, that nobleman insisted on justice being done, so with an ill-grace the amount (something over sixteen pounds sterling) was paid up. A poor enough fee for risking one's life in battle!

At this period MacIntyre was in the employ of Breadalbane, engaged as a keeper on the Glenorchy hills and deer forests. Here, in the freedom of the hillside and glen, he composed his verses, probably repeating them aloud until he had them to his taste. And when we remember that

he was an old man before he could even read, and that he
never learned to write, that feat is to me at least rather more
than noteworthy ! On two poems composed about this
period much of his reputation rests : " Mairi Ban Og,"
or " Mary the Young, the Fair-haired," and the well-known
song-poem of " Ben Dorain."

In 1793 MacIntyre joined Breadalbane's Fencibles,
in which he was given the rank of sergeant. He served
with that force for some six years, indeed, until the regiment
was disbanded. He was now a veteran of seventy-five, and
out of employment. Of course, his clean, open-air life,
inured to all weathers and hardships, meant that even at that
age he was not yet ready to sit by the fireside, his life's work
done. Far from it, indeed, and so the Earl of Breadalbane
again used his kindly influence, and Duncan MacIntyre
obtained a position in the City Guard of Edinburgh. The
pay was sixpence a day ; but the poet appears to have been
well content with his lot, and found time amidst his duties—
probably far from onerous—to compose more than one
set of verses.

Duncan carried a musket and acted as a guardian of
the peace until his eighty-second year. In October, 1812,
he passed away in his eighty-eighth year, and was buried
in Greyfriars churchyard.

Throughout his long life, Duncan Ban MacIntyre's
heart was ever in his native Glenorchy. A few years
before his death he visited his beloved glen for the last time,
and wandered over the hills he knew and loved so well.
To-day he is not forgotten, nor is he likely to pass from
memory so long as Highland hearts beat.

One afternoon I happened to be in Dalmally, waiting
rather vainly for a 'bus, because the snow, still falling, was
already deep. Accompanied by a gillie, I had been satisfy-

ing an old desire to cross Glenorchy when snow wreathed the hillsides. We arrived in Dalmally in the early afternoon, and were enjoying our smoke after a hot meal, waiting for the means to get to Crianlarich station. The only other occupant of the hotel parlour was an old man, white-bearded and weather-beaten. It was obvious from his halting remarks that he spoke little English, and my gillie had even difficulty in following his Gaelic.

This veteran told us that he had lived in a cottage on the hillside all his days, and was on one of his rare visits to the town. " Ask him," I said to the gillie, " if he ever heard of the Macnabs, the famous smiths who lived here and whose family history goes back to the building of Kilchurn ? Yes, was the answer, he remembered the last of the family, but that was more than fifty years previously. He was halting and uncertain ; and then his eye brightened as he recollected something, and he commenced talking in a quick, excited tone, difficult to follow. My friend made him repeat slowly, going over it all again once or twice, but even then we were unable to make much of it. His Gaelic had subtly altered from the speech of to-day, and was difficult to follow.

It appeared that my chance enquiry about the Macnabs had stirred some forgotten chord in the old man's memory, and he was pathetically anxious to tell us what he knew. Again and again my friend drew him up and made him repeat his words. In broken sentences he told us that one day Duncan Ban MacIntyre had been out on the Glenorchy hills, and observing a goat with a peculiar horn, had shot it and brought the trophy to Macnab the smith to have it mounted as a *sgian dhu*. Macnab was a noted craftsman, and, proud of his commission from the poet, made it a thing of beauty. When payment was proffered, the smith refused, asking instead that Duncan Ban should compose a verse upon the weapon !

These were the words of the verse, so far as we could get their meaning, halting enough in English, but doubtless beautiful as the poet conceived them in the original Gaelic :

> " To-day I got my choice of a knife,
> New from the fire well beat ;
> Now it has a goat's horn handle—
> The goat last night lay in the
> rock with the springs."

The " rock with the springs," I believe, refers to a place in Glen Lochay.

This old man remembered the rotting stumps of the gallows, relic of the old MacGregor days when the glens were the heritage of that fighting clan—but the poet was nearest his heart.

And so it is with most of us. The sweet singers linger long in the hearts of a nation, and in Duncan Ban MacIntyre the Gaelic-speaking people have a heritage rich and full.

# PEDEN THE PROPHET

NO stranger figure has flitted across the pages of Scottish ecclesiastical history than Alexander Peden. In that stern chapter which recounts the doings of the Covenanters, he was the most subtle, elusive personality of all the men who placed conscience before worldly inheritance; his name comes uppermost to the mind. Even now, although many generations have passed since his day, and perhaps in many ways the stress of modern life has altered the outlook and softened the fibre of his successors, the name of Peden the Prophet carries with it a halo of romance and reverence in most of our South-Western parishes.

A gaunt, tireless man, to whom physical want and well-being were mere empty phrases. Count him a fanatic if you will; laugh at his misdirected enthusiasms if that be your type; but do remember that all that is best in the old Scottish character, everything that Scotland stands for in the outer world to-day, was moulded and formed by just such undeviating, ruthless strength of mind.

Right or wrong, Peden carved his own way in life, and followed it to the bitter end, knowing what it meant, but keeping straight along the path he had planned, refusing to be driven from his cherished beliefs even if the result should mean death by martyrdom. Narrow-minded as he was stubborn, foolish if you will, immolated upon a cause which meant nothing to other people of at least as fine spiritual outlook—even so, I believe that Alexander Peden, to the Scottish race, is like a lantern in a dark place, and for his strength of character alone is to-day worthy of our homage.

How to describe him physically? Perhaps that paragraph in *The Tale of Tod Lapraik* might serve, because R. L. Stevenson had an uncanny pen when it came to drawing a picture of this sort. "In thir days, dwalled upon the Bass a man of God, Peden the Prophet was his name. Ye'll have heard tell of Prophet Peden. There was never the wale of him sinsyne, and it's a question wi' mony if there ever was his like afore. He was wild's a peag hag, fearsome to look at, fearsome to hear, his face like the day of judgment. The voice of him was like a solan's and dinnled in folk's lugs, and the words of him like coals of fire."

Of course, R.L.S. was not the only teller of tales to feature Peden as a character. From Allan Cunningham onwards, the Prophet's rough-hewn features have peeped at us from between the covers of the literary man, either under his own name or disguised, as becomes the writer's art. S. R. Crockett, in more modern days, too, delineated Peden : " A strange man, his long grey beard falling deep on his breast, tall far beyond the ordinary height of mankind, his hair thrown back from a broad brow, and in his eyes a strange cast—the look of the second-sight, the inner vision of things unseen."

It is not as a mere prophet embalmed in a novelist's pages that this man of iron will is here introduced, but rather as a Scot—a fellow countryman—to whom perhaps we owe more than we realise, or than I, in my space, can endeavour to make clear. Prophet, saint or fanatic—whatever one's measurement decides for him—Peden began life like any normal laddie of his times. It is generally accepted—one cannot be meticulously accurate with such trivial details in the Scotland of three hundred years ago—that he was born in the little farmhouse of Auchincloich in the parish of

Sorn, in the year 1626. The district is a bleak one and wind-swept, lying on the borders of that rough moorland country which forms the boundary of the parishes of Sorn and Galston. In Peden's time it would be virtually inaccessible. A foot track would probably conduct to the path—it *might* have been a roadway—which led to Sorn Castle and the wider worlds of Kilmarnock, Ayr and the older villages.

The surroundings into which Peden was born, geographical and social, judged by even a poor standard to-day, were in any case, uncouth and uncomfortable. Yet his people must have been of that hard-working, good-living class which has played such a part in the development of our land merely by that urge to rear their families in the faith and above all see that they were educated and so fitted to take their place in a wider sphere. Where Peden received his early training is not clear, but certain it is that he attended Glasgow University. Like most lowland Scots of his day and class, he was reared in an atmosphere of strict spiritual faith. His staunch moral outlook, brooding tendency, and the benefits of a superior education, fitted him for one career—the kirk, the hope of most lads-o-pairts in outlying districts until perhaps a generation or two ago, when new developments and wider outlook enlarged the view.

Even so, his first appointment was that of schoolmaster in Tarbolton. There he combined that duty with the offices of precentor and session-clerk. According to Woodrow, he later acted as precentor of Fenwick kirk, but that is doubtful. Perhaps the confusion arose from the fact that the minister of Tarbolton in Peden's time was the Rev. John Guthrie, whose brother, a man more widely known throughout the church, was William Guthrie of Fenwick.

James Guthrie, the Stirling martyr, was a cousin. Amongst so many divines of like name a slip is excusable.

But Peden's heart was in the church, and in due course he was elected minister of the little Galloway church of New Luce. For three years he ministered to his scattered parishioners with whole-hearted devotion, beloved by all for his fire and eloquence. But his peaceful years were not to last, and his sowing in that secluded field was to yield a strange harvest. A storm was about to break over the kirk and upon all who decided to remain true to their conscience and faith. Peden, who asked for nothing but to be allowed to live his peaceful days in his quiet parish, was faced, as a sincere man, with no alternative but to join in the revolt against the high-handed, intolerant fiat of the government.

He was ejected from his church under the terms of what was known as " The Drunken Act of Glasgow," because, as a historian tells us, " the members of the Council were all so drunk that they were not capable of considering anything that was put before them "—a sad commentary on the times and methods employed by the classes in their ruling of the masses !

This Act was passed in 1662 by the Privy Council sitting in Glasgow. Its essence was to the effect that all ministers who had not been inducted to their charges prior to 1649 and who had not submitted to the authority of their bishops, must " remove themselves and their families *out of their parishes* (the italics are mine) betwixt the first day of October and the first day of November next to come, and not reside within the bounds of their respective Presbyteries." Further, they were to be deprived of all stipends, including that for the current period. If any minister resisted, the military were instructed to enter his church and forcibly remove him from his pulpit.

That was the position which faced Alexander Peden at New Luce in 1663. He had two options, but not for one moment did he hesitate upon his course of action. So he entered, as did many another, upon a life of hiding in caves and moss-holes, of hill conventicles and meetings where armed men acted as sentries to give warning of the approaching dragoons. Ministers in those days were dreich, and Peden was no exception. His farewell service in New Luce seems to have been prolonged until darkness fell. At the close of this service, he appears to have first manifested his power of prophecy, or divination, call it what you will. As he left his pulpit for the last time, on closing the door he gave it three solemn knocks with his Bible, and three times he repeated the words, " In my Master's name, I arrest thee : that none ever enter thee, but such as enter as I have done, by the door." That was in 1663. The " period of unrest," as I will call it for lack of a non-controversial term, lasted for some twenty-five years, and during that time no " indulged " minister preached from that pulpit or even entered its door !

And now came that part of his life, twenty years of wanderings as a legal outlaw, which placed Peden's name amongst the immortals in the chronicles of our land.

His acts were naturally obnoxious to the government of Charles II., and so he was officially " put to the horn," and a reward was offered for his person. His crime was that he had baptised children, performed the marriage ceremony, and addressed meetings, contrary to the law. He was also officially named as having " ridden up and down the country with sword and pistols, in grey clothes." How foolish and pedantic those old proclamations read to modern eyes ! But it was no joke to Alexander Peden. His life, nay, more, his hope of aiding and assisting his fellow men and women

THE FIELD PREACHING.

was at stake, but he was wary as he was guileless, clever as he was meek. He often went disguised in wig and mask, and there was a signal whistle or call which conveyed warning to the initiated.

Shortly afterwards came the ill-fated Pentland Rising, which failed so signally, at Rullion Green. Again Peden manifested his eerie power of peering into the future. He joined the little army and marched with them as far as Lanark, but after warning the leaders that failure would be their portion, he declined to continue. No man who reads his record can accuse Peden of cowardice. On the contrary, he was a very brave man, but one endowed with a measure of commonsense and clear thinking, with an ability to place facts in their logical order and to foresee results, a faculty obviously lacking in many of the Covenanting leaders. The brain to conceive plus the power to act logically according to circumstances are not obvious Scottish qualities. Not merely was the power wanting among the Covenanting divines ; the same lack of foresight was the undoing of the '45 and betrayed our country's army on more than one field of greater national importance.

Peden's wanderings for the next year or two are naturally obscure and difficult to follow. We hear of him in Ireland, come across traces of him in England even ; but mostly he was living and ministering amongst his own folks in the West, exhorting them to stand firm, comforting the bereaved, and generally maintaining the spirits of his fellows, and so becoming every day more obnoxious to the king's party.

In Ayrshire, particularly, there are many Peden's caves and pulpits. Wherever he went, the hunted, persecuted Covenanters gave his name to the stone used as a pulpit or to the ford which he had crossed, so that to-day,

C

in a manner surprising to the city dweller, the traditions, even the admonitions, of the man are fresh and alive.

Oftentimes the mist would come down and save him when Dalziel's troopers thought he was in their power. On one occasion he himself, at grave personal risk, guided a party of dragoons across a ford, although had they guessed his identity his life would have paid forfeit. He was afraid that the only other guide who could show them the way, a young boy, might be frightened or bullied into disclosing some information. As to the enveloping mist just mentioned, there are several authenticated instances of Peden praying for protection when hard pressed, in company with aged or infirm—*and his prayers were never unanswered*. To disbelieve that statement is to disregard the solemn testimony of men and women who had no fear for themselves and no need to make the statements if untrue. Readers of that wonderful book, *The Psalms in Human Life*, by Prothero, will gain an insight into Peden's life as viewed by an English divine and man of letters. They will find that Peden is credited with "not only the temperament but the training of the seer."

At last the wanderer was captured, at Knockdow, and was taken as prisoner to the Tolbooth of Edinburgh. He was imprisoned on the Bass, and there remained for more than four years. From there he was taken again to the Tolbooth, and fully a year later was sentenced to banishment. He was to go as a slave on the Plantations, a fate meted out also to many of his followers.

When embarked at Leith, Peden comforted his fellow prisoners by promising that they would never be taken overseas ; they were to be of good cheer, for deliverance was at hand. The ship duly sailed for London, where the sixty or more prisoners were to be re-embarked upon another vessel for Virginia. When the London skipper ascertained that his prisoners were not mere criminals and law-breakers, but sincere, good-living people, he refused to take them on board. The Leith captain had fulfilled his contract, the London skipper was obdurate, and so the prisoners were set free to go where they willed! Peden went back to Scotland, leaving his traditions in the Border country on his way home. But years were passing, and although not an old man, he had experienced a life of constant battle against man and nature. Hunted and tracked, living and oftentimes sleeping exposed to mist and rain, cold and discomfort, with insufficient food and scanty clothing, he crept home to his own countryside to die.

He dared not enter a house for any period, and so found shelter in a cave. The cave is still there, to be seen by any-one who cares. It is situated, a mile or two from Mauch-line, in the Auchinleck estate. It is a mere hole in the high, rocky bank of the Lugar, and the only method of ingress or egress is to use the roots of an ancient oak as a ladder. To visit it is a precarious experience. The cave is more difficult to leave than to enter, and the visitor had better not turn his eyes below at the rock-strewn river bed when engaged in the adventure—all his faculties should be employed on the task on hand.

From there, Peden, now conscious of his end, crawled to his brother's house, where he died on January 26, 1686. He was buried in Auchinleck kirkyard, but was not even allowed to rest unmolested. Six weeks later a party of dragoons dug up his coffin, tore off his shroud and draped it upon a nearby tree. His body was taken to Old Cumnock, where it was to be hung in chains on the gallows, but the Earl of Dumfries and some other influential persons inter-vened to prevent this outrage. The body was accordingly buried at the gallows-foot. Others expressed a wish to be interred near Peden, and so in time the spot once unsightly with its hideous burdens became the local churchyard. There we leave Alexander Peden in the peace and repose which he never enjoyed in life.

One of my regrets is that, many years ago, as a child in a little Ayrshire village, I witnessed the burning of a small volume because it had become ragged and dog-eared. It was the Prophecies of Alexander Peden, by whom collected and published I have never ascertained. To-day that book would have had a cherished place on my bookshelves. But life is like that.

**LITHGOW IN THE LIBYAN DESERT.**

" The Soyle we daily traced was covered with hard and soft Sands, and them full of Serpents . . . Jackals, Beares, and Boares, and sometimes Cymbers, Tygers, and Leopards.''

# WILLIAM LITHGOW

## Traveller and Poet

WILLIAM LITHGOW is well worthy of his place in our gallery. Indeed, of all the personalities sketched or still to come under the scalpel, he is most fitted for the appellation " quaint." Born in Lanark, sometime towards the closing years of the sixteenth century—probably 1582—he was educated at the Grammar School there, and it speaks well for his old dominie that in such dark and difficult times he so thoroughly equipped his pupils. Why Lithgow left his own country and embarked upon the travels, upon the records of which his reputation rests, is a little difficult definitely to ascertain. One tradition is that he was in love with a Miss Lockhart, and when the affair came to the knowledge of the lady's people, her brothers vindicated the family honour by assaulting Lithgow, and, amongst other deeds, cutting off his ears. It was an uncouth period in our country's annals, and such a thing might well happen. While Lithgow came of good stock, it was perhaps more " bonnet laird " than aristocrat in quality, and the lady was some degrees higher in the social scale than her swain. His father was a Burgess of Lanark, and appears to have been proprietor of the small estate of Boathaugh, situated not far from the county town.

Young Lithgow, as we have seen, had received a particularly good education for a country lad of his time, was well versed in classical literature and doubtless considered himself a person eminently suitable to mate with the Laird of Bonnington's daughter. Her brothers thought differently, and so, to quote his own words, he was fated to become a victim at the " hands of four blood-shedding wolves, fairly devour, and shake in pieces one silly straggling lamb !   Yea, and most certainly, that unawares, the harmless innocent unexpecting evill may suddenly bee surprized by the ambushment of life betraying foes."

To a young man of spirit, one whose people were of a certain minor importance in the district, such branding, as the loss of his ears, was hard to bear.   It was a coarse age, and the milk of human kindness did not flow too freely in the veins of his peasant neighbours.   The fact that he was so brutally disfigured, the reason for the deed, were food for jest and humour, and he became known as " Cut Luggs."   Here, then, was reason enough for turning his back on his native town, and setting forth in quest of adventure in scenes where the cause of his humiliating experiences were unknown.

Whatever the reason that prompted him to become a wanderer, it marked him for all time as that notable person —*the first Scotsman to write a book of travel*.   How many have since followed his example in that respect is a literary conjecture, but he was the leader, the pioneer, and as such is a noteworthy man and one whose career we must examine!

His first excursion was a visit to Orkney and Shetland, no very outstanding feat to-day, but then as far off the beaten track as is the most remote South Sea island in our time.   Next he crossed to the Continent and made a " thorough survey " of Germany, Switzerland and the Netherlands.   His experiences on these grounds merely whetted his appetite for more unknown lands and peoples, and in 1609, while still a lad in his early twenties, he set out from Paris for Italy.   He left the French capital on March 7, and forty days later arrived in Rome.

This " way-faring journey," as he terms it, was accomplished on foot. If his observations on Paris were none too complimentary, indeed he considered it " a masse of poore people, for lacques and pages, a nest of rogues, a tumultous place, a noctuall den of thieves, and a confused multitude," he was no more graceful in his remarks about Rome. In his eyes the Rome of that day was a mere shadow of the imperial city of past times, "now only the carkas of the other, of which she retaineth nothing but her ruines, and the cause of them, her sins."

Whatever the reader's judgment of William Lithgow may be, in my opinion he was a stout fellow. His contempt for the " vermillion Nymphs " and his refusal to accept a seat in a " Caroch " because he preferred to walk the long miles and find out all that was of interest, are much to his credit.

After many wanderings and excursions in the Adriatic, Lithgow took ship from Raguso on a vessel bound for Corfu. On leaving the island on a Greek boat after a day or two at sea, the captain sighted a ship approaching, and on sending a look-out man to report, it was ascertained that the stranger was a Turkish galley. The passengers, a mixed collection of Greeks, Slavonians, Italians, Armenians and Jews, were now overcome by panic and the bulk wanted to surrender without resistance. Not so William Lithgow, who pointed out to the captain how he in any case stood to lose his ship, and so he ought to put up a fight. Pikes and firearms were served out, and a fierce battle waged until dark, when the Turk drew off, to re-engage again with day-break. A storm arose, and the Greek ship, sorely stricken, escaped from her more powerful enemy. From Greece to Crete, the Ægean Islands ; the Dardanelles and Constantinople, then to Syria, Palestine, Egypt, and home to

England was no mean itinerary in those days, and well worth writing about at a time when even a journey from Scotland to London was an event, and marked a man as far-travelled. In any case, the story of these adventures formed his first literary effort, and duly made their appearance. But the wanderlust was now in his blood, and he was soon off again in quest of further rare sights and experiences.

Throughout his works we find him being robbed by evil persons or unjustly fined by high-handed authorities, and while he uses those facts as texts for expounding to his readers the wicked minds of such as live by banditry, the truth of the matter is he was not above committing an act of roguery on his own behalf when opportunity offered.

Considering his high moral tone, it is amusing to read of one adventure in which he was chief actor. It was during his second visit to the Continent, and having parted with a friend who was intent upon returning home, Lithgow was "traversing the Kingdom of Trapani, seeking transportation for Africa." He was unable to find a ship, and, recollecting a nobleman who had befriended him on a former occasion, he decided to visit this friend and also make a call upon another young nobleman in the same neighbourhood, the two castles being some eight miles apart.

Next morning he "marched by the breach of day," and then met with some good "lucke." The "lucke" to which he refers was that while travelling through a lonely part of the country, midway between the two young noblemen's estates, he came upon them both lying dead, their horses securely tied to some low trees. They had fought a duel about a lady, and were so evenly matched, that each had mortally wounded his opponent. And now William Lithgow exhibits himself in a very bad light. He approached the two bodies, and, finding them richly garbed in silks and fine stuffs, he searched their pockets and discovered two silken purses " full laden " with gold. He also removed five valuable rings from their fingers, and, searching for a suitable spot, hid the booty. Next, mounting one of the horses, he galloped off to appraise his host of the previous evening, who at once took the sad news to the castle. Soon a concourse of relatives and retainers of both houses arrived on the scene, when Lithgow, retrieving the cash and rings, proceeded on his way ! Nothing could be more cynical than his description of his action, and " to save the thing that was not lost," he that day travelled thirty miles before resting, and next morning took sail for Malta. There he found a London ship and had a drunken carousal with some of the crew. Thus did Lithgow fall from grace, and one is entitled to doubt his moralising on other occasions !

That incident probably altered his itinerary, and we follow him by divers ways to the Sahara. There we find him lost in admiration of blacksmiths who were forming horse shoes, nails and so on from cold iron, the metal being made malleable by the " raies of the Sunne." He would have imparted further information on this subject, but suddenly he remembered that " Time, Paper, Printing and charges " would not allow of any expansion on the theme !

Sooner or later we all meet trouble in this world, and William Lithgow was marching towards his fate. On his third visit to the Continent he was arrested in Spain and handed over to the Inquisition. There he underwent tortures almost too horrible to dwell upon but for his own gusto in recounting his sufferings. That he suffered cruelly there is no doubt, and he describes his pangs and pains most graphically and at some considerable length. At last news of his predicament got out, and he was handed over to a British Admiral who came ashore for the purpose with an armed force.

On being conveyed home to London, Lithgow's physical condition as the result of the tortures he had suffered in Malaga, excited considerable interest. He was a broken man, in body at least, because his mind, as his history proves, was still active enough. The King interested himself in the case, and on two occasions sent Lithgow to Bath for treatment, personally defraying all expenses. The Spanish Ambassador to the English Court promised to exert his influence and obtain reparation, but it was obviously lip service and nothing was ever done. Time passed, and Lithgow's hopes from that quarter began to fade. When the Ambassador was due to leave England for his own country, Lithgow contrived to meet him in the royal apartments, and commenced to rail and reproach him for failing to carry out his promises. Words led to blows, and, crippled as he was, the Scot appears to have inflicted considerable punishment on the Don. This was too serious a matter to be overlooked and hushed up, and so he was sent to prison and remained in the Marshalsea for some nine months. While he later appealed to the Government to intercede and obtain for him the promised indemnity, it is not on record that he met with any success.

He appears to have made a wonderful recovery from his Malaga experiences ; indeed he must have been an extraordinary man physically. On being freed from prison he made his way home to Scotland. Chambers tells us that he lies buried in Lanark churchyard, and terms him " a strange compound of good sense, fanaticism, impudence and pedantry." He goes on to inform us that when the great traveller returned " maimed and disfigured by the

Inquisition of Spain," he settled in his native parish, where he was known, and was there still remembered by the name of Lugless Willie Lithgow. This authority may be correct in his statement that Lithgow lies interred in Lanark Kirkyard. The Statistical Account bears him out, furthermore stating that no trace of his grave remains. Even so, and in face of such authorities, the question may be permitted to stand as doubtful. He certainly did not settle down at home, but continued his wanderings for several years, as his printed works conclusively prove. He was released from the Marshalsea in 1623, and in 1637 appeared his " Siege of Brada," followed in 1643 by his " Survey of London," and then in 1645 by his " Siege of Newcastle." By this date—remember that he was born about 1582— he must have been a man well on in years, and there is no record, that I can find, of his return to Lanark. It is not an important point really, but it is all too vague to be precise on either dates or facts.

Not merely did Lithgow publish travel and adventure books. He was also a poet, and his collected verses were issued some sixty years ago. Only one hundred copies were printed, and I am the happy possessor of a volume which originally belonged to a distinguished professor, and has passed through other hands before gracing my shelves.

It is rather hard going in parts, somewhat deficient in places, but more than one piece is of value as a picture of the times. The most interesting—and that is merely individual opinion—is a poem. " Times Sorrowful Disaster of Dunglasse." This piece contains " infallible grounds and reasons, how that most execrable and parracidiall deed was committed." The verses chronicle one of those deeds so impossible for sane minds to understand were they not historically vouched for. The scene is

Dunglasse and the date August, 1640. The Earl of Haddington was in residence, surrounded by guests and retainers,
among others his English page, a boy named Edward Paris.
One evening the Earl, in jovial mood and probably talking
at his youthful page with intention to tease him, was ridicul-
ing the English for losing the battle of Newburn. In a rage,
the page boy seized the heavy kitchen poker from off the
fire and, running to the powder magazine, thrust the red
hot iron into a barrel. The magazine contained some
eighteen hundredweight of powder, and the result can be
imagined. The castle was blown up, many were killed.
About sixty bodies were recovered, while :

> The rest (unfound) ly terrd, corps,
>     clothes and bones,
> Under huge heap of glutenated
>     stones.

The Earl of Haddington and his brother ; Colonel
Erskine, a son of the Earl of Mar : John Keith, son of the
late Earl Marshall, with some knights and lairds, including
the Lairds of Inglistown and Gogar, and some army
officers were among those whose bodies were recovered.
The exact number who perished was never fully ascertained,
although some few did escape, notably

> Young Dalmahoy, and happie Prestongrange,
> Who by heaven's marv'lous mercy, in this change,
> Did wondrously escape ; and yet both wounded.

Read, not in verse, but as a mirror of the times, Lithgow's words are interesting as throwing light on the customs
and outlook of the period in which he lived.

And so let us leave William Lithgow, something of a
mystery man, traveller and poet, or, as he described himself, " the Bonaventure of Europe, Asia and Africa."
He was a virile character and had he lived three hundred

years later, would have been a prince among War Correspondents. As it is, and as already mentioned, he was the first Scot to publish a record of his travels abroad, an example followed by many of his race, and one doubtless to be perpetuated by succeeding generations still to come—for which example, the reader must bless or curse him according to his lights !

# SIR ROBERT GRIERSON

## The Laird of Lag

THE hand of time wipes everything clean. Even the sordid, brutal Covenanting episodes—well named the " killing-time "—can be viewed to-day by the most rabid partisan, with a measure of cold blood. The old tales are dying out with the generations as they pass. The old stones that record the martyrs in so many country kirkyards are becoming defaced and illegible by reason of time and weather, and call mutely for another Old Mortality if they are to survive. In more than one God's acre the memorial stones are moss-grown and gradually sinking into the ground as if they would mingle with the very dust whose names they strive to perpetuate. On the hillsides the pulpit rocks are losing their identity amongst the younger people ; erosion is undermining caves and hideholes which were almost held sacred in the days of our grandfathers.

Even Nature would seem to be taking a hand in silently effacing the fell traces of a time perhaps as well forgotten but for its lessons to those who have minds so attuned, or its legends to the lover of old tales.

But there are some names that will never be forgotten so long as a kirk bell rings and freedom of conscience survives in our land. Of these men, a few names are writ in bolder letters, but all are etched deep in the scroll of the Scottish church. Debit and credit, they are there for all to see. Such men as John Knox, Richard Cameron, Alexander Peden and Donald Cargill, to name a few at random. Men who dared to raise their voices against overweening authority, and who, without exception—and as they well knew would be the case—suffered because of their temerity.

On the other side were men of quite as strong character, determined to carry out the instructions of those in authority, ruthless in their disregard for human suffering so long as duty—as they saw it—lay along that path.

Claverhouse—a fine soldier, a born leader, fearless in battle and adored by his men. He is either a dastard or a brilliant, dashing cavalry man—according to your angle. Dalyell of Bins, a torturing bloodthirsty creature, who introduced the *thumbikins* from Russia, cold-blooded enough to strike a defenceless prisoner on the face with the hilt of his dirk. After the murder of Charles I. he refused to shave his beard, because of some self-imposed vow, and at the period under review it was down to his girdle, a white, unkempt mass of fuzzy hair.

These are two I place on the debit side of the country's ledger—but, let us remember, if they were brutal and callous towards every human feeling when opposed, they were merely the servants of their Government. Their actions were not a whit worse than those of the Hanoverian troops during and after the '45. Perhaps not quite so brutally callous as to-day's use of poison gas or the dropping of bombs on open towns. It was a species of warfare— troops against peasants admittedly, but all such force is equally brutal, a mixture of mud and blood, and generally arises from weak or faulty government. Remember the Glencoe nightmare was practically contemporary, and you will admit the seventeenth century was a black period in our national life.

Some men seem to have been born for just such episodes. They revel in the bloody work to their hand and go about it with enthusiastic zest.

I do not think Claverhouse relished his task, and I am quite certain no covenanting leader—and there were fools and clowns amongst them, too—but loathed and abjured it all. There are varying shades in human personality. Some are light, others grey, while here and there we come across one of a darker hue. In the subject of this sketch we meet one of a definite black.

Perhaps it is unjust, but the more I study Grierson of Lag the more convinced I become that he was a foul bully, a man of spiritual insensibility, who delighted in his ghastly work.

From Dumfries to Carsphairn, from the trackless Galloway hills to the Wigtown coast, the Laird of Lag has monuments aplenty in tribute of his deeds. His name appears in doggerel verses on many headstones—odd and whimsical but for their deep sincerity—testifying that the dust they guard was placed there before their due time because of his blood lust and almost inhuman ferocity. Strong language, I know, but justifiably so on this man's record.

" The family of Grierson," to quote Francis Grose, " is descended from Gilbert, the second son of Malcolm Laird of McGregor, who died in 1374."

The subject of our sketch was the last of his race to occupy the old castle of Lag in Nithsdale. The ruined walls of the old stronghold still remain. At one time it was surrounded by an outer wall, and was apparently encompassed by a lake, which latterly became an undrained morass, and, again according to Grose, who visited it fully a century and a half ago, " must, even in its best days, have been a damp and dreary mansion." One interesting thing that Grose tells us is that at Barnside Hill, Sir Robert Grierson, " exercised his prerogative as a baron of the regality and barony of Lag, by trying, condemning and hanging a sheep-stealer. This is said to have been the last instance in Nithsdale of a criminal suffering death by sentence of a Baron Bailie." Of course, we have no complaint with Lag on that score. Sheep-stealing was an offence punishable by death throughout the land, and Sir Robert could salve his conscience—if it ever gave him a twinge—with the truth that he was merely putting into operation the law as it appertained to the case.

As a matter of fact, Grierson was a model laird to his own tenants, and for all his cold-blooded ferocity there was a rare streak in his nature as witnessed by the couplet he endorsed on his rent book :—

> " O Lord, we're aye ganging and we're aye gettin' ;
>
> We should aye be comin' to Thee, but we're aye forgettin.' "

These two lines would have made an apt epitaph for him, because they almost sum up his life and character.

Old customs die hard, and there was one known as " playing Lag " which flourished in this part of the country until comparatively modern times ; indeed, in more remote districts it may still be occasionally perpetuated.

On a dark evening, preferably about Hallowe'en when warlocks and witches roam the countryside, a gathering would be convened in some appointed kitchen. While the wind shrieked and moaned round the house and byre, the assembly would regale each other with tales of Lag and his killings. All the old, half-forgotten incidents would be recounted, each more gruesome than the previous, the only light the flickering peat fire. One of the party would meanwhile be busy in another apartment donning a disguise to impersonate the part. Then the door would slowly

D

open and a horrid figure creep into the room, searching, as the play demanded, for the Covenanters there assembled. Suddenly some individual was pounced upon, while the others, worked into an emotional condition by the tales and atmosphere created, although they well knew the ritual, were frozen to their seats. The victim would struggle until the disguise was disarranged and disclosed some well-known face. Then the lamps were lit, and jollity and fun took the place of the sombre atmosphere. Perhaps it may appear childish to the reader, but think of the reputation of the man whose deeds were so perpetuated even in a ploy!

Of course, much of the tradition handed down is, as we shall see later, mere romance, but the record is black enough if we merely recount authentic facts.

Sir Robert Grierson was born somewhere about 1650, and does not appear to have been active in the earlier episodes of the Covenanting period. The position as it was before his entry upon the scene seems to be that the Government was baffled in its efforts to suppress field conventicles. Bands of Highlanders, still known as the " Highland Host," were brought from their native glens and quartered in the Western Counties. To the native peasantry, they were a source of terror. Their rough and uncouth appearance, the fact that few of the invaders could speak aught but Gaelic, that they were there by order of the Government and given practically a free hand to ravish and pillage, an opportunity of which they took full advantage, is to our modern eyes an almost unbelievable spectacle. But such are the facts. The Highlanders looted and despoiled the lowlands, returning to their homes laden with plenishing and gear to such an extent that the territories which suffered from this invasion of human locusts were impoverished for more than one generation.

Even these extreme measures had not the desired effect, and the people still continued to hold their meetings undaunted and undismayed. Still stronger efforts were called for if the Covenanting movement was to be suppressed. Extra troops were ordered to the scene, and Dumfries, Lanark and Ayr became in a measure garrison towns.

The above is the merest outline of the state of affairs which sets the stage for the appearance of our chief actor, Sir Robert Grierson of Lag.

Sir Andrew Agnew deputed Claverhouse and Sir Robert Grierson as Sheriff-deputes with full authority to quell the people's meetings; they were also appointed justices of the peace, so that their powers were unquestioned. To follow Lag in his wanderings would now be merely to recount a series of cold-blooded murders, particulars of which are open to anyone who has a desire to investigate. Howie informs us, too, that, in addition to shedding blood, Lag imposed fines in Galloway and Nithsdale amounting to £1200—a vast sum considering the times and social conditions.

Apart from the sordid shootings and butcherings, the record of which is chronicled in type and on the headstones erected throughout the district, there are two episodes which denote the man and his methods.

One February morning in 1685, Lag and his troopers came upon John Bell of Whiteside and three other men on Kirkconnel Hill in the parish of Tongland. Lag knew Bell intimately, and yet would not even allow him fifteen minutes to prepare for his end. On that request being made, he raved at him and asked if " he had not had time enough to pray since Bothwell ? " Not merely were the men shot out of hand, but Grierson refused to allow their bodies to be given burial. A short time after this event,

Viscount Kenmure challenged Lag with his unnatural conduct in refusing to allow Bell's remains to be interred. Sir Robert's reply was an oath and the remark : " Take him if you will and salt him in your beef barrel." Kenmure drew his sword, and would have slain Lag in his rage had not Claverhouse come upon the scene and averted the deed.

The other example I shall comment upon is what is to-day known as the " Wigton Martyrs," in recounting which Wodrow says, " History scarce affords a parallel to this in all its circumstances." The facts are familiar to most, but this sketch would be incomplete without a reference.

Gilbert Wilson was a well-to-do farmer at Glenvernoch in the parish of Penningham. As a matter of fact, the crown had no justifiable cause for complaint against him. To quote Wodrow again, Wilson "was every way conform to episcopy ; and his wife without anything to be objected against her, as to her regularity." Even so, at some times a hundred troopers were quartered on his lands, eating his substance and destroying his gear. Practically once a week for some years he had to appear in court to the neglect of his own affairs. A man of substance, he was harried and plundered to such an extent that he died in poverty, while his widow had to subsist on charity.

This man had two daughters who at the date in review, 1685, were aged respectively 18 and 13 years. An acquaintance, whom they believed to be a friend, one Patrick Stewart, met the children—for such they were—in Wigton, and proposed that they should adjourn and drink the king's health. The children demurred, and Stewart lodged information against them. They were at once apprehended and lodged in the " thieves' hole," but later transferred to the gaol, where they found Margaret McLaughlan, a woman then upwards of sixty years of age. There was no fire, no bed, and the food supplied was scant and poor.

The three prisoners were ultimately brought up for trial before Lag and some others, charged with taking part in Ayrsmoss and Bothwell Brig'. The trumped-up charge was criminally absurd. The children could not possibly have taken part in these affairs, and the widow had never been within many miles of either place. Their pleas were rejected, and all three were sentenced to be tied to stakes within the tide-mark of the water of Blednoch near Wigton and there to be drowned. Agnes Wilson, the thirteen-year-old child, was reprieved on payment of £100 sterling by her father. Every reader knows the harrowing tale of how the other two were done to death before the sorrowing people who were unable to avert the act.

Those two instances are alone sufficient to brand the Laird of Lag as a monster. If, to the sum of his misdeeds, you add only the authenticated misdeeds which stand against his name, you have a record unworthy of any civilised human being.

Lag was not to get passing through life unscathed, and we find that Lord Kenmure arrested him in his own house and had him lodged in Kirkcudbright gaol, from whence he was transferred to Edinburgh Tolbooth. This was in June, 1689, and my authority states that he was released in August on giving surety for peaceful behaviour. If that is so, his liberty did not endure for a lengthy period, because in March, 1692, we find him appealing from Cannongate Gaol on the plea that he " was contracting some ailments under protracted confinement." His imprisonment was probably of a preventive character, as the Privy Council were in a highly nervous condition through

Jacobite plots, and, of course, Lag would naturally be suspect by William's ministers.

Four years later he was again in trouble with the authorities. This time the charge was " clipping of good money and coining of false money." This charge merely shows the lamentable ignorance of the times. What actually happened was that Lag had let his house at Rock-hill to a person named Shochan, who was engaged in cloth-stamping. A suspicion arose that coining was being engaged in—Lag's enemies would naturally believe any-thing against his reputation—and although a search was made and no incriminating evidence discovered, such was the gossip and clamour, that the prosecution was proceeded with ! The charge broke down when heard in Court, but Grierson was worried and upset.

Most readers will agree that Wandering Willie's tale in *Redgauntlet* is one of the most graphic stories ever penned by Scott. Lag Castle is Redgauntlet, and Grierson is the prototype of the weird figure round whom Sir Walter wove his romance. It is too long to quote here, but Scott got his material from Train, who was familiar with it as part of the lore of the Nithsdale countryside.

Lag died at the age of 86, in December, 1733, at his town house in Dumfries, and there, too, old tales of his memory linger. He suffered from gout, and in his last illness his shrieks and imprecations were heard in the street. Servants were continually carrying pails of cold water to ease his burning pains, but whenever his feet were plunged into the water it commenced to boil. When he made to drink a glass of wine, it congealed into blood at his touch. Absurd, of course, but they show the atmosphere which surrounded the man.

The night of his death was wild and stormy. A small

ship was making her way towards the Solway and battling against the fierce hurricane, when the lookout spied a strange apparition making to cross her bows. Every man aboard was terrified at the sight which met his eyes. It was a huge black coach equipped with torch-bearers and out-riders, and it was driving across the angry waters at full gallop. The skipper, bolder than his men, hailed the coach and asked its destination. " From hell for Lag," was the muffled response as the coach drove by.

Lag had grown so corpulent that it is said part of the wall of his house had to be taken down to allow his coffin to be taken out. But even in death the weird tales sur-rounded his name, and when the cortege was on its way to the kirkyard at Dunscore, after proceeding for a little way, the hearse stopped. Strive and struggle as they did, the four horses could not pull the load. Sir Thomas Kirkpatrick was one of the mourners, and, swearing that he would have the hearse moved no matter what fell power objected, he sent for his own horses, a notable team, and harnessed them to the coach. Whipping them up, he drove to the churchyard at a gallop—where on arriving his steeds dropped dead !

As I say, these are mere local romances, gathered round a figure which in the eyes of his countrymen typified all that was evil and wicked.

# JOSEPH TRAIN

## Sir Walter's Friend

JOSEPH TRAIN appeals to me as having been, in every sense of the word, a unique personality. He was a man of marked ability, and one who worked to the limit of his resources. It is undeniable that his name will never be forgotten so long as the Waverley Novels are read; yet by the same token, for all his personal abilities and endowments, his energy and enthusiasm, we can only class him as a brilliant failure.

Perhaps that is a hard judgment, but it is, I think, a just one, inasmuch as Train might have left us a legacy equal to that of, say, John Galt, but for the fact that he chose to help others rather than to make a name for himself. We all know a someone, blessed with intellectual ability, who would rather fill in his time doing all sorts of unnecessary or unrequited jobs for other folk than concentrate on his own appointed task.

Of literary ghosts there are many. In a Fleet Street bar you will find men qualified to write with authority on almost any subject. But Train does not exactly come in that category. He was rather a provider of information in an entirely voluntary capacity, one who felt deeply honoured by the kindly friendship of Sir Walter Scott, and whose enthusiasm for the cause, to quote a phrase, brought its own reward. My complaint against him is that he ought to have written more himself, and turned his abilities to greater account.

Train was born in 1779 in the Ayrshire village of Sorn, not far removed from the birthplace of Alexander Peden, the subject of a previous sketch. It is surprising how

richly endowed that western district is in men of outstanding character and ability. A glance at the gravestones in
the old kirkyards will reveal to a discerning eye more than
one interesting literary association, and near here, too, the
house still stands, although slightly altered in status, in
which Burns " dinner't wi' a lord."

But Train did not spend many of his early years in
his native village, and while he was still a child his parents
removed to Ayr. There he received his schooling—
education is hardly the term—and as a youth of twenty,
when the Ayrshire militia was being formed and recruited
by ballot in 1799, his lot was to don uniform and serve his
country. The term exacted was three years or the duration
of the war, and as in those days we were mostly at war with
our neighbours across the Channel, he might well have
spent a goodly part of his life guarding our coasts. As it
happened, the peace of Amiens brought him freedom to
return to civil life in 1802. His regimental duties were not
onerous, and as he devoted his free time to study and self-
improvement, these years were perhaps employed to better
advantage than would have been the case had he been
allowed to spend them under his father's roof.

The regiment was for a period stationed in Inverness,
and while there our militiaman observed an advertisement
of Currie's edition of Burns, and determined to possess a
copy. Placing an order with a local bookseller, Train
arranged that the book should be held for him until he had
paid up sufficient instalments to redeem his purchase.
Without resources apart from his pay as a private soldier,
this entailed considerable sacrifice.

And then one of those unexpected incidents which so
often shape our future brought Train prominently before
the notice of the one man who could do most to help him

in life. Sir David Hunter Blair was commander of the regiment, and on visiting the bookseller's shop he observed the new edition of Burns. He was interested, asked the price, and expressed his wish to buy the volume. On being told that it cost £1 11s. 6d., that a copy could be obtained if he so wished, but that this special volume was reserved for one of his own men, he was naturally astonished. But his surprise took the practical form of instructing the bookseller to have the work bound in the best possible style and at once delivered free of all cost to Train, the full expense to be charged to Sir David.

Nor was that all. As the militia were on the eve of being disbanded, the commander exerted his influence and obtained for his protégé the Ayr agency for James Finlay & Co. Train entered upon his new duties with his usual whole-hearted enthusiasm. Here was the type of young men worthy of help and encouragement, so Sir David again used his influence and was enabled, by enlisting the sympathies of the Earl of Eglinton, to obtain for him an appointment in the Excise.

In 1811 Train was formally instructed to take up duty in Largs. Two years later he was promoted to Newton Stewart, a district rich in lore and natural beauty. This new environment formed the bent of his mind, and from then on he was collecting old tales and traditions of Galloway and Carrick, enriching his mind and developing that natural aptitude for study and investigation which was to enlarge his outlook and bring him into close contact with at least one of the greatest men of our race, Sir Walter Scott.

The year 1813 must have been a busy term for our Exciseman. Not merely did he carry out his normal duties with assiduity, but he found time also to transpose

**JOSEPH TRAIN.**
A Silhouette Portrait.

much of his traditionary lore into verse, and in 1814 he published his first volume, *Gleanings of the Mountain Muse*. Apart from the poems, the book is valuable to us to-day because in his footnotes the author preserves much other-wise-to-be-forgotten legend. As was to be expected at that time, the little volume was issued from Edinburgh. Scott, with his wonderful *penchant* for discovering all that was going on around him, happened to read some of the proofs, and put his name down for several copies. He wrote a flattering letter to the new-found poet, and this started a corespondence and led to a friendship mutually valuable.

Scott's interest was no empty one, and he evinced a desire to help in a practical way by pointing out in what manner Train might improve his literary craft. This was instanced particularly in a letter from Abbotsford, dated July, 1814, in which Sir Walter advised Train that he was leaving for an extended tour abroad and purposed making the volume of his poems his close companion.

In that letter Scott made a suggested alteration to one of the poems on which Train's final reputation rests. The criticism illustrates the keen insight and vivid imagination of the great novelist. The poem in question is *Elcine de Aggart*, founded on a tradition of the Spanish Armada invasion of 1588. Elcine de Aggart was a Carrick lady, known locally as a witch, and she turned her gifts to advantage in protecting our shores from the Spaniards.

Scott's criticism was that one line was faulty. He hoped that the author would see fit to amend it in any future edition. Here is the verse as it stood :

They bring with them nobles our castles to fill,
They bring with them ploughshares our manors to till ;
They likewise bring fetters our barons to bind,
<u>Or any who they may refractory find.</u>

   But this mighty clue
   Of the indigo hue,
While few, like de Aggart, could e'er understand,
Will baffle their hopes ere they win to our land.

The fourth line, here underlined, is the one to which Scott took exception, and he suggested instead the line :

They bring with them yokes for the neck of the hind.

Those who will trouble to read the verse again, and to substitute the new line for the original, will, I think, agree with me that the hand of the craftsman gives a new life and character to it.

Train's book contained much out-of-the-way lore, because he was not only a collector of tales and legends, but had the additional faculty of weaving them into his own work and of giving them an added interest because of his ready pen. Among others, The Warlock Laird of Fail (a strange personage whom we will meet in a later article), A Cabal of Witches, The Hag of the Heath, and so on, give an indication of how he turned to good account, and preserved the dying traditions from former times.

There died in 1710 a well-known Carrick gentleman, head of a great house, whose active participation against the Covenanters gained for him amongst the western peasantry the title of " Sir Archibald the Wicked." Train introduced this semi-mythical figure into his work, and added a lengthy footnote touching on the supernatural.

Sir Walter Scott, always quick to note and appraise, took the facts and used them for " Wandering Willie's tale " in *Redgauntlet*.

When engaged upon his *Lord of the Isles*, Sir Walter wrote to Train, making a request for any help he could supply for that work, and at the same time thanking him for his interesting collection of legends. The result of the request was a journey to Turnberry on Train's part. The success of his research may be found in the footnotes to *The Lord of the Isles*. Perhaps it is not too much to claim that *Guy Mannering* owed its origin to the old ballad resurrected by Train, who took it down from the lips of an old lady in Castle Douglas, and sent it to Scott. Sir Walter, in his introduction, gives a somewhat different origin, but Lockhart is inclined to favour the other view.

But Train did not exhaust his energies in the collecting of old tales and ballads. He was instrumental in obtaining a considerable number of curios, relics of supreme interest to a mind like that of Waverley. Among other articles which he sent to enrich Sir Walter's " chamber of horrors," as someone termed it, was a drinking horn provided by Bruce for the use of the lepers at King's Case ; a battle-axe found in Cree Moss ; a spearhead unearthed near Peningham ; a peculiarly formed razor, a product of the fifteenth century ; and—what was perhaps of more genuine interest to the recipient—Rob Roy's sporran.

Scott invited his correspondent to visit him, and Train made the journey to Edinburgh in the early summer of 1816. He was received and treated with every show of kindly consideration, as befitted an honoured and welcome guest. Scott gave a dinner-party and invited more than one celebrity who he thought might interest or help his Ayrshire friend.

A chance remark by Train bore valuable fruit.     Sir Walter and Train were in the library and the Exciseman was remarking upon the somewhat mild expression of Claverhouse, whose picture hung upon the wall.     Sir Walter defended Claverhouse against the ecclesiastical historians of the period, and Train ventured to suggest that he would make a fine figure for a romance —as interesting as Wallace or Bruce.     Let me quote Train's account of what followed :

" Seeing that the subject somewhat pleased Sir Walter, I added, ' and if the story was delivered from the mouth of Old Mortality—in a manner somewhat similar to *The Lay of the Last Minstrel*—it would certainly heighten the effect of the tale.'     ' Old Mortality :     Man :     Who was he ? ' said Sir Walter hastily, his eye brightening at the same time ;  and I will never forget the intense anxiety he evinced whilst I related briefly all the particulars of that singular individual I could then recollect.     I promised, immediately on my return to Galloway, to make every possible enquiry respecting him, and to forward the same either to Abbotsford or to Edinburgh without the least delay.     He said he would look most anxiously for my communication ;  and he spoke these words so emphatically as to leave no doubt on my mind that the information required was for the purpose of being published. . . .    Proud of the kind reception I had met with in Edinburgh from Sir Walter, I returned to Galloway, resolving to use every means in my power to serve him, by collecting traditionary stories of every description, but more particularly, what related to the Covenanters and to Old Mortality."

With what result the world to-day knows.    When in London in the following year, Sir Walter met Chalmers, then actually engaged upon his *Caledonia*.    He strongly advised the historian to communicate with Train before completing his work, more especially in connection with Galloway, explaining that he personally was indebted to his correspondent for interesting accounts of the " Murder Hole," the " Pict's Kiln " and other legends of that district. The result of this suggestion was a lengthy correspondence and much valuable data and assistance for the *Caledonia*. Chalmers had never heard of " The Deil's Dyke," and Train, who introduced it to his notice, spent his leisure hours tracing the dyke for a stretch of almost eighty miles. So thorough was he that he examined the charters of every estate through which the dyke ran. That Scott was duly appreciative of the help given by Train is exemplified in a letter from Chalmers, dated from Whitehall, August, 1819, which closes with these remarks *a propos* Galloway : " " ——the romance which is so attractive in the hands of our friend Walter Scott, and for which, I am informed, you have supplied many materials."

Every one interested in the traditional story of Scotland is, or ought to be, familiar with Chambers' *Picture of Scotland*, and that being so, must have made the acquaintance of Sir Ulrick Macwhirter. I do not propose to recount that strange legend of Blairquhan here, but merely to mention that it was rescued by Train and given to his patron, Sir David Hunter Blair, who in turn presented it to Robert Chambers for inclusion in his now famous volumes.

In Scott's *Tales of a Grandfather* the author gives us some interesting particulars about Donald Nan Ord, Donald of the Hammer. The facts were sent to Scott by Train, who had received them from a doctor then practising in Newton Stewart, and at one time located in Appin.

Notwithstanding the time occupied by his investigations and correspondence with the great, Train did not neglect his professional duties, and in 1820 he was promoted to the position of Supervisor. This preferment was due in great measure to the influence of Scott, but shortly afterwards it involved his leaving Galloway and taking up house in Cupar-Fife. At once he got busy prying into the legendary tales of his new surroundings. He so roused the enthusiasm of his fellow excisemen that soon all the members of his staff were keen on tracing old tales and other lore—an enthusiasm which became slightly unbalanced. One incident distressed Train very much. An assistant, anxious to help, went to Falkland Palace and stripped the chair of James IV. of its carvings, which he sent to his superior with an account of their interest and value !

Scott was so interested in Train's Fife notes that he visited the district in person to examine some ancient crosses, the result of which was *McDuff's Cross*.

From Fife Train was moved to Kirkintilloch, where he still continued his research, and amongst other things forwarded to Abbotsford some Roman remains from Castle Carey. Next he was appointed to Queensferry, and this brought him into still closer touch with Scott. At the Wizard's request he commenced collecting all sorts of anecdotes and customs from amongst the fishermen, and some of the results of his labours found their setting in *Quentin Durward*.

But an exciseman's life—in those days at least—appears to have been a rather unsettled existence ; at any rate, Train was again moved, this time to Falkirk. And again the Abbotsford museum profited by the new location. The bow of Sir John Graeme, who was slain at the Battle of Falkirk in 1298, and two quaighs, one made from a piece of Wallace's oak in Torwood, the other from a section of the yew which flourished above the grave of Graeme, were welcomed as treasures in the Border home.

Some fancied neglect, which appears to have been but a venial offence, brought about a reduction in office, and Train was transferred to Dumfries. There he settled down contentedly and again proceeded to combine his official duties with the congenial task of searching out old lore. Amongst other contributions from Dumfries, the " Fire Raid," " Kimstrie's Willie " and " Wild Man of Dinwiddie Green " found their way to Abbotsford, and in addition some notes which were used in *The Fair Maid of Perth*. Later, at Sir Walter's request, were forwarded accounts and notes upon the originals of the characters whom Scott named as Dick Hetterick and Meg Merrilees ; and some anecdotes about Marshall, the King of the Gypsies.

Sir Walter made public acknowledgment of the help contributed by Joseph Train in, amongst other instances, *Old Mortality*, *Guy Mannering*, *Peveril of the Peak*, *The Heart of Midlothian*, *The Surgeon's Daughter*, *The Lord of the Isles*, and *Chronicles of the Canongate*. Train was proud to help the illustrious novelist without fee or other gift, and the mutual friendship brought its reward to each.

It is good to record such a single-minded enthusiasm as that displayed by the subject of this sketch, because there was nothing of the sycophant about Joseph Train. He was a man of a clean, open-air type, and when his day for withdrawal from active service arrived, he retired to a cottage near Carlinwark loch, there to indulge in his hobbies and fancies until the day dawned when he, too, was to become a memory and a legend.

Perhaps his character and impulses are best understood in some lines from his own pen :

E

> I've loved thee, old Scotia, and love thee I will,
> Till the heart that now beats in my bosom is still.

Joseph Train died in 1852, having led a full and busy and therefore happy life. By virtue of his association with the distinguished author of the Waverley Novels his name will never be altogether forgotten while a love of clean literature survives. What might have been had he worked and created on his own accounts, who can say?

**HENRY MACKENZIE.**
A Contemporary Portrait.

# HENRY MACKENZIE

## The Man of Feeling

IT will not be seriously disputed that to-day we are prone
to run to type. In kirk or senate the ability may be
present, but the marked personality is definitely amissing.
It is not a matter of dress, although there, too, we have
become uniform in style. It is rather a lack of colour,
of atmosphere, and it becomes more apparent as the years
pass.

A short time ago I was discussing the subject with a
fellow-traveller in the Royal Scot. He, too, had observed
this gradual change, and he pointed out that a few years ago,
to quote his own words, " the horsey man, the professional
man, the plumber, and the farmer—all were easily recognis-
able in the streets, but hardly so to-day." Perhaps that is a
rather sweeping statement, but I am not so sure that,
broadly speaking, he was not quite right. Indeed, on the
following day, and in the same Glasgow street, I recognised
two well-known Glasgow divines, one dressed in a lounge
suit and coloured tie, the other attired in plus-fours and a
cloth cap.

There is nothing wrong in that, of course, no objection
whatever in a semi-free country such as ours is to-day ;
but their garb definitely marked these clerics as members
of the crowd, nothing more or less—and it helps to prove
my point.

To live in retrospect is bad : the future is what matters
most to all of us ; nevertheless a Scottish gentleman of the
eighteenth century, if he rose above mediocrity and ever

ventured furth of his own fields, was, or at least *looked*, an individual of defined personality. And it is period that the reader is asked to consider at the moment. The Edinburgh of the late eighteenth century was one of the most interesting cities in Europe. A coterie of literary men, brilliant and self-assured, graced the capital and founded a reputation for their city which lingers to this day. It was Smollett, I think, who said that Edinburgh was a " hotbed of genius."

The leading man of his time, the pivot of the witty, cultured community, was Henry Mackenzie. He was a genuine son of Auld Reekie, born in the city he loved so well and did so much to adorn. His father was a leading physician in a centre famous for its medical men, and his mother was a daughter of Mr. Rose of Kilravock, then, as now, one of the outstanding Scottish county families.

This being his pedigree, young Mackenzie was ushered into the world with one priceless asset if he could use it aright—an assured position in society. The date of his birth is one easy to remember, because he was born on that August day in 1745 which saw Bonnie Prince Charlie land on the West Coast. Those were harassing times for Scotland in general, but nowhere more so than in the capital, the natural objective of the Highland army. Whatever the state of the city when Henry Mackenzie was laid to rest there some eighty-six years later, his entry into the world found Edinburgh in a troubled state. The citizens were divided in their allegiance, the castle was watchful and uneasy, the very ministers entered their pulpits with swords concealed beneath their black gowns.

The Old Town was almost entirely surrounded by walls, and the New Town, the Edinburgh of to-day, was as nature created it—green fields and furzeland. Princes

Street was the Lang Dykes, along which Claverhouse had galloped only a comparatively few years earlier on his way to the Highlands. The beautiful gardens which now add such charm to the view were then the Nor' Loch. Twenty years later—in 1763—Ross Park was sold for £1200, to blossom subsequently into George Square, where doubtless the ground annuals of this day far exceed the original purchase price. The stately Mound, which now leads up to the High Street, was a deep morass, and the present ridge was formed by throwing the ground open as a " free coup " for the earth and debris dug up in working the New Town foundations. If born into a rather dirty, almost callous environment, Mackenzie lived to see the progressive spirit then awakening alter and change his city until to-day it occupies a position of proved eminence.

It was here, then, in that small, clarty, wall-enclosed town that young Mackenzie lived his boyhood years and received his schooling. Sometimes it is difficult to understand how refinement and culture could develop in these surroundings. So late as 1773, when Henry Mackenzie was a man of twenty-eight, the great Dr. Johnson visited Edinburgh with his shadow, Boswell, and as they were walking up the High Street at nightfall, the biographer asked the philosopher if he could see his way. " Lead on," the gruff old bear replied, " I can smell you in the dark." The pleasant custom of emptying slops and refuse from the windows with a warning cry of *Gardyloo !** and an absence of sanitary and cleansing services, probably accounted for that harsh pleasantry.

There was no incentive to reform in the public mind ;

* A corruption of the French warning, in similar circumstances gardez l'eau—" beware of the water."

people were then more inclined to accept conditions without agitating for improvement. The view was narrow, self-centred. Henry Mackenzie was a lad of thirteen years before any regular conveyance linked Edinburgh with Glasgow, then a thriving town with a population of some 35,000 souls. When the service was started, the coach took twelve hours to cover the forty odd miles, and a break for dinner was imperative. William Creech, in *Edinburgh Fugitive Pieces*, published in 1815, notes with obvious pride the fact that " a person may now set out on Sunday afternoon, after divine service, from Edinburgh to London ; may stay a whole day in London, and be again in Edinburgh on Saturday at six in the morning : The distance from Edinburgh to London is four hundred miles. Forty years ago, it was common for people to make their wills before setting out on a London journey."

I hold the view that to appreciate a man and his work at their true value it is at least desirable to know something of the times and conditions in which he existed. That is why I have given the reader a skeleton outline of the environment in which Mackenzie lived. The point is that Scotland generally, and Edinburgh in particular, was becoming more enlightened, wider in outlook, and during the years from 1753 to 1757, when he was attending the High School, the dark shadows of the previous century were fading, the repression of John Knox losing its grip. The convivial life of club and tavern was growing, and the church was dividing into two sects—those of moderate outlook and the puritanical " unco guid " to whom Burns later gave the death blow. No incident illustrates this cleavage more aptly than the production of the play, *Douglas*. That drama was the work of John Home, a minister, be it noted, nd the uproar which followed its appearance split the classes into two camps. This was in 1756, and gradually Edinburgh was improving intellectually.

In 1757 Henry Mackenzie left school and was enrolled as a student at the University. He pursued his studies there for four years, terminating in 1761, when it was decided that he should enter the legal profession, and he was duly articled with a city firm. His special branch was to be Exchequer practice, so, in order to gain more experience, he went, in 1765, to London, where he worked at his, profession for three years before returning again to his native city. In the quiet, studious youth no one appears to have observed any marked ability such as was to blossom at a later date.

In 1771 there was issued a novel, *The Man of Feeling*, which met with instantaneous success. It placed the author as one of the leading writers of his time, but it was anonymous, and few had the secret of its origin. Some time after the book had taken its indisputed place amongst the great works of the decade, a clergymen in Bath claimed to be the writer, and so forced the rightful author to acknowledge his work. From then onwards Henry Mackenzie became known to an ever increasing circle of intimates and admirers as " The Man of Feeling," a rather unfortunate soubriquet for the cool, hard-headed man of business who was rapidly making his position secure in the legal community. He had been assumed as a partner with his old firm, and indeed succeeded his senior as Crown Attorney. Later he was appointed Comptroller of Taxes for Scotland, a position which demanded more hard-headed acumen than his literary outpourings would convey. A second book, *The Man of the World*, made its bow to the public in 1773 ; in the same year a play, *The Prince of Tunis*, was produced in Edinburgh, and four lears later came another work from his pen, *Julia de Roubigne*. None of these last, however, achieved any great measure of success. Mackenzie was author of several other comedies and tragedies, including *Spanish Father*, *Force of Fashion*, *White Hypocrite* and *Shipwreck*, or *Fatal Curiosity*. Lawyer, successful novelist and playwright, poet of sorts, he had a social standing which may be measured in the fact that in 1776 he married a Miss Penuel Grant, daughter of Sir Ludovic Grant of Grant, chief of that clan.

Mackenzie had a ready pen and must have been a man of boundless energy and fecundity, because, notwithstanding his legal duties, his endless social functions, he contrived to be continually writing articles and sketches. Many of these fragments appeared in a weekly journal, *The Mirror*, which he originated and edited during its lifetime of fully a year. His next venture was *The Lounger*, inaugurated in February, 1785, which ran with more or less success for about two years.

To a Scot this latter venture holds a peculiar interest. Robert Burns had been in Edinburgh for a week when *The Lounger* for Saturday, December 9, 1786, made its appearance. Of the poet's genius and ultimate position there is no shadow of doubt, but at that time, although known and appreciated for his poems and songs in his native territory, his fame had not yet spread abroad. Moreover, he was depressed, somewhat in the shadows, and was pleased to share the humble lodgings of a poor lawyer's clerk, an old Mauchline acquaintance, at a weekly rent of something about half-a-crown.

As an offset to this picture, compare the position and influence of Henry Mackenzie. A man-of-the-world, cultured and refined, leader of the most brilliant literary set in the capital (I almost wrote " Europe," and would not have been guilty of exaggeration), influential to a degree. Burns, on the contrary, was an unknown Ayrshire plough-man, fired with the divine spark of genius, it is true, but as yet with the mud of his native fields hardly brushed clean from his boots. In ability the men are not comparable : Burns is an immortal ; but let us face the position as it then existed.

And then appeared this issue of *The Lounger*, mentor of the social and intellectual group, with an eulogistic article on the ploughman-poet from the editor's pen. It was headed, " Surprising effects of original genius, exempli-fied in the Poetical Productions of Robert Burns, an Ayr-shire Ploughman." The article was an appreciation of the Kilmarnock edition, and the closing note was a hope that something could be done to prevent the poet from carrying out his intention of going to the West Indies.

The effect was instantaneous, and the result is common knowledge. But even then Mackenzie did not rest. His interest was genuinely aroused, and he acted as adviser to Burns in his negotiations with Creech for the disposing of his rights after the first Edinburgh edition had been published. When the Bard set out on his Highland tour he was armed with letters of introduction to several of Mackenzie's friends, amongst others his brother-in-law, Sir James Grant of Grant.

Lovers of Burns owe a considerable debt to Mackenzie, and the Colinton Burns Club showed their appreciation when at their annual dinner in 1931, on the centenary of the death of The Man of Feeling, a proposal was made to erect a memorial plaque commemorating his residence in South Cottage in Colinton. The project was put into being, and the then Edinburgh Lord Provost, Sir Thomas Whitson, duly unveiled the memorial, paying a well deserved tribute on the occasion.

As already mentioned, *The Man of Feeling* was published anonymously; and strangely enough the author's name is associated with another and a greater novel, also issued under the veil of anonymity.  When Scott wrote *Waverley*, the first edition, published in 1814, was dedicated to " Our Scottish Addison, Henry Mackenzie, by an unknown Admirer of his Genius."

These two facts alone serve to illumine the name of Henry Mackenzie and assure for him a place in the hearts of all who have any regard for Scottish letters.   To be the first person to draw attention publicly to Robert Burns, and to have had *Waverley* dedicated to his own name, is surely tribute enough for any man, and signifies a personality out of the common rut.

Mackenzie's works were issued in three odd little volumes, in 1818, from the press of William Blair for John Dick, bookseller, High Street, Edinburgh. These lie before me as I write, and interesting reading I find them, but not of a type likely to find favour to-day.   They are " dated " in subject, matter and style, so far as modern taste is concerned, but, even so, I can promise any one who takes the trouble to secure them that some pleasant hours are awaiting.   Even in the choice of names for his characters Mackenzie is apposite and happy.   Colonel Caustic, Lord Grubwell, Barbara Heartless, John Homespun, Rebecca Prune : these are names that fit their parts admirably ; indeed, one intuitively thinks of Dickens or Thackeray, so much is each name a mirror intimately portraying the part it is made to play.

Allowing for all that, I do not think that the written works of The Man of Feeling will ever again become popular with the reading classes. Students of literature, and persons interested in the period, will find them illuminative. Even the J. M. Dent issue of the book so peculiarly associated with Mackenzie's name, published in 1893, was limited to one hundred copies for this country, and fifty for America. My own copy is number forty-eight, and it had passed through two or three hands before I purchased it.

There is one point, however, which I can venture to assert—that Mackenzie's name will never be forgotten. Round the city of Edinburgh has grown a veritable literature. The books on its annals, romance, old streets and associations still pour from the printing press, and it is a thin volume indeed that does not refer to Henry Mackenzie and account some anecdote or reminiscence associated with him and with his times. That, of itself, will for ever keep his memory green, and tempt an odd reader to enquire more closely into the record of the man. Even without knowing his works at first hand, most readers are aware that he was amongst the first—if not really the first—to encourage Burns. His association with Burns and Scott we know, but also Thomas Campbell and Pollok were both indebted to his kindly interest. He was in great measure responsible for the pension bestowed on Mrs. Grant of Laggan. Amongst his friends he numbered Viscount Melville, Adam Smith, William Pitt, and Hume. In his day *Blackwood's* and the *Edinburgh Review* were something more than national institutions, they occupied a place which we to-day cannot fully realise.

Lord Cockburn refers to Mackenzie more than once in his *Memorials*, and in one place he writes of him as " one of the *arbitri elegantiarum* of Old Edinburgh. . . . In person, he was thin, shrivelled and yellow, kiln-dried, with something, when seen in profile, of the clever, wicked look of Voltaire." Lockhart also gives us a description of him in his home circle, but he compares Mackenzie's physical likeness to Warren Hastings. These two pictures were drawn when the subject was an old man, mentally vigorous notwithstanding his burden of years, but even so, changed and altered from the keen, alert literary man of affairs whose example created a law amongst the elite of his day.

Mackenzie survived until 1831, and died at the ripe age of eighty-six, almost the last representative of that Golden Age which stands for so much in Scottish letters. He was interred in Greyfriars kirkyard, that hallowed ground where headstones to-day remind us of so many vivid chapters in our national life.

A man who lived through the most interesting period in his city's annals, Henry Mackenzie was acknowledged leader in all he undertook. If he personally does not rank as a great writer—and I would not concede the doubt if he be judged by his contemporaries—he undoubtedly, by help and admonition, encouraged more than one to enter the ranks of the immortals, and by so doing laid posterity under a real debt of gratitude. He was a man whose life mattered.

THOMAS CAMPBELL.

# THOMAS CAMPBELL

## Poet of St. Mungo

A GOOD many years ago, when as a lad I was employed in a Glasgow office, my employers subscribed to some political fund or other, and so always received a ticket for the St. Andrew's Hall gatherings. My recollection is that there were more assemblies of the sort in those pre-war days, or perhaps the type of politician then in power paid more attention to Scottish affairs. I do not know ; but my feeling is of frequent large gatherings and of statesmanlike utterances to enthusiastic audiences, and of crowds unable to gain admission blocking the streets and impeding the traffic.

Even with a reserved seat I was always early, because of the musical programme which prefaced the arrival of the platform party. The Arthur Balfour choir rendered various songs and pieces to entertain the great audiences, and one of their masterpieces was *Ye Mariners of England.* How the audience used to thrill when the organ surged above the vocal pitch and the vast volume of sound as everyone took up the chorus ! To a young lad it was a memorable occasion in days when cinemas and wireless, motor 'buses and aeroplanes, were unknown quantities ; but even as I see it now, after a lapse of some thirty odd years, it was a fitting prelude as a means of tuning up the emotions and so assuring the proper atmosphere for the speaker of the evening. Stage management, perhaps ; but it was robust, manly stuff—every air as the composer meant it to be rendered, familiar to all and thoroughly

enjoyable.   But even then I used sometimes to wonder
how many of the enthusiastic vocalists knew or cared, when
they joined in and almost drowned the large choir, that the
words which they obviously knew so well, and which had
such a moving appeal, were written by a Glasgow man—
Thomas Campbell.

Professor Nichol, speaking at the unveiling of the
Thomas Campbell statue in George Square, Glasgow, in
1877—exactly one hundred years from the poet's birth—
expressed the opinion that *Ye Mariners of England* was one
of the three greatest war songs ever written, the other
two, according to the professor, being the *Marseillaise*
and *Scots Wha Hae*.   The man who wrote any one of these
did not live in vain.   Even if his name fades from public
memory, his words are immortal in the hearts of the
liberty-loving peoples.

Thomas Campbell, then, was a Glasgow man, although
many city folks do not appear to recognise the fact ;  indeed,
poets, with a few notable exceptions, are somewhat akin
to prophets, in that they have no honour in their own
country.   But if Campbell is unfamiliar to many of our
busy citizens, I am just as certain of the fact that if he could
return to his native haunts he would not recognise the town
of his birth.

Least of all would he know the site of the College of which
he was three times Lord Rector, on one occasion outvoting
Sir Walter Scott for the honour—and than that I can produce no greater measure of his stature in the eyes of his
contemporaries.   To-day the scene of his triumph is a
busy goods station, with a never-ceasing stream of horse
and motor lorries laden with merchandise for the four
quarters of the earth.   The stage coaches of his time have
given place to electric cars and 'buses, and the very street

in which he was born would strike him as more foreign than any town or city visited during his European travels.

It was on July 27, 1777, that Thomas Campbell first saw the light in the High Street of Glasgow. He was the tenth and youngest child of his father, who at the poet's birth was a man of sixty-seven years. The family had fallen on evil days. At one time the Campbells were of some small importance, in the then thriving business community, in that branch of commerce known as Virginian merchants; but the American war brought disaster and failure to many, amongst others Mr. Campbell, who lost fully £20,000 by his commitments.

To modern eyes, the Glasgow of the poet's boyhood years would appear a strange, uncouth place. Like all large centres, Glasgow owed its place and progress to the fact that it acted as a magnet to young men anxious to get on in life. Clever and energetic lads found no opening for their ambitions in the villages and small towns, but the wealth and opportunities of the city held out tempting baits. The Campbells came from Kilmichael-Glassary, between Inveraray and Ardrishaig, and Thomas Campbell, if actually Glasgow born, is another name which may almost be added to the line of outstanding poets in which that district has been so prolific.

One sometimes wonders how it was possible to create delicate verse, even to make any pretence to culture, in such an age and amongst such a people. Indeed, for some years—roughly, the latter half of the eighteenth century—Glasgow degenerated. True, it was a passing phase; but it was into this vulgar, hard-drinking community, with its lack of restraint only equalled by its lack of amenities, that young Campbell was born. A town of some fifty thousand citizens, Glasgow was in that "hobbledehoy" stage of growing too quickly to have full control of its limbs. Many of the old landmarks are gone—necessarily so ; but here and there an ancient building still serves to remind us of that other Glasgow, now a memory.

The gateway to the College, bearing the date 1658, was removed to the modern University ; and of its near neighbour, the Tron Church, only the tower remains. In the closing period of the eighteenth century, when Campbell was a lad of sixteen years, the Tron Church was set on fire by some young men and completely destroyed. At that time the city guard was composed of public-spirited citizens who took it in turn to patrol the dark streets. Their headquarters was the Session room of the Tron kirk, and a large fire was kept going so that they might have some comfort when coming off duty.

One dark night, or, rather, early morning, in 1793, the guard as a body went out to patrol the town, leaving the kirk door unfastened. As chance would have it, a number of young men—probably the actual cause of the guards' absence from the premises—members of an association known as the Hell Fire Club, returning to their homes after a night's debauchery, and observing the open door and inviting fire, entered the Session room. To keep the fire going, and in a spirit of drunken bravado, they broke off certain seats and benches and added them to the flames. Soon the room became so stifling that they were compelled to go outside, and the draught from the open door, fanning the flames, in a few moments made of the church a blazing mass.

That one incident illustrates the social side of Glasgow when our poet was a lad—the hard-drinking, untamed outlook, which, palliate it as you will, undoubtedly existed in every grade of society.

Even so, amongst a section, there was a real love of letters ; and uncouth as life was, at least, to our modern eyes, Scotland generally was forgetting the Covenanting times, the '45 and all the other incidents which retarded national prosperity and under a new free-trading system with England, the Union of 1707 was bringing material prosperity and progress in its train.

When he attained the age of eight years, young Campbell was enrolled as a scholar at the old Grammar School. There he was in good hands, because Mr. Allison was a capable teacher and a man who took a personal interest in each youth entrusted to his care. The boy's father, too, now a man well on in years and no longer immersed in affairs, made it his pleasure to assist and tutor his Benjamin. Soon Thomas took a leading place in the class room, and in Latin and Greek especially he excelled his fellows. Of an open, frank disposition, the boy became a general favourite alike with teachers and scholars ; but unfortunately his studies took toll of a constitution not any too robust, and he was sent into the country for a time to recuperate. Pollokshaws, where he was sent to reside in the cottage of an old weaver, was then a mere clachan, and roving the fields or wandering on the banks of the Cart imbued him with a love of nature which was to tincture his whole life.

His childish schooldays past, Campbell was entered as a student at the University, and once again his brilliant parts achieved high place. His early grounding in Greek and Latin now proved invaluable, and in place of prose he worked his exercises in verse. When but a boy of thirteen he had one of his poems printed and sold to his fellow-students at a penny per copy. Indeed, as a lad he produced some remarkable verse, and when only sixteen years of

F

age he wrote a hymn, *When Jordan hushed his waters still*, an outstanding composition and a gauge of his poetic genius.

With all his diligence as a scholar and his erudition in the classics, he was a very human boy. When seventeen, and pursuing his brilliant career at college, he was responsible for a cantrip which brought smiles to more than one grave face. At this period—1795—an apothecary named A. Fife carried on business in the Trongate. The wearing of earrings was then fashionable amongst the ladies, and the apothecary had a notice on his window : " Ears Pierced by A. Fife." By a coincidence the next door shop was a public house and the owner was named Drum. The two merchants were not at all on friendly terms. The humour of the position appealed to Campbell's lively imagination, and one dark evening (there were no street lamps in those days) the youthful poet, with two willing friends to assist, fixed a long board across the front of the two shops, with the painted inscription :

> The spirit-stirring Drum,
> The ear-splitting Fife.

Campbell was discovered as the author of this humorous outrage and was severely reprimanded by the authorities.

Financial difficulties were now casting a shadow on the Campbell household, and the youthful poet decided to lighten the burden while still pursuing his University studies. With this end in view, he obtained a position, during a recess, as tutor to a family in Mull, and in May, 1795, accompanied by a friend, he set off on foot, tramping by Inveraray to the Western seaboard. His sojourn amongst the wild hills and moorlands helped to form his mind and gave birth to imaginings the value of which posterity has gleaned.

In 1796 Campbell completed his course of study and left the University, and again he secured a post as tutor, to a family in Argyll. But the literary urge was at work and led him to Edinburgh, where he was engaged by some publishers. Hack work and tutoring kept him provided for, but every free moment was devoted to an ambitious task, none other than the writing of *The Pleasures of Hope*. At last, when its author was in his twenty-first year, this book was issued from the press, and soon the poet's name and reputation were assured. Edition followed edition, and other verses strengthened his position amongst the cultured classes.

Campbell was now planning another volume, *Queen of the North*, and in 1800 sailed from Leith for Hamburg, to improve his knowledge of German and obtain material for his pages. He was warmly received there by British residents, his fame having preceded him, but, unfortunately, war was in the air and he was advised to proceed to Ratisban, as being a safer place in which to reside. It was anything but peaceful, and he witnessed the French troops driving the Austrians before them through the streets of the town. He saw also the charge of the Austrian cavalry; the battle of Hohenlinden, however, so associated with his name, he did not see, but relied upon his imagination for his description.

When war was declared between this country and Denmark, Campbell's plans were finally upset, and it was with no little risk that he ventured to return to Leith, his vessel being chased by a Danish ship and just escaping by putting into Yarmouth. Finding himself landed in England instead of in his native land, he changed his plans and proceeded to London, where he was warmly welcomed by Perry of the *Morning Chronicle*, whose columns had been open to him for some time. It was no empty greeting either, for the London editor took Campbell under his protection, encouraged him by kind words and deeds, and introduced him to many eminent literary men in the English capital. Two new friends almost vied with each other in their efforts to assist the poet—Lords Holland and Minto. The latter invited Campbell to take up residence for a time in his town house in Hanover Square, an offer which the poet wisely accepted. Here he met the lions of the pen and the stage, leaders in society, in fact, the most brilliant intellectual coterie in London.

The new and illustrated edition of *The Pleasures of Hope*, with the addition of some hitherto unpublished verses, was issued in June, 1802, and proved a complete success, so much so that the author's feeling of insecurity was now banished. In September of that year he carried out his dearest ambition, and was married in St. Margaret's, Westminster, to his cousin, Matilda Sinclair of Greenock, whom he had first met when on his way to Mull some years earlier.

Campbell was now offered the Regent's Chair in the Russian University of Wilna ; but his bent was literary work, and against the advice of his titled patrons he refused the office. Financial worries, not entirely of his own making, now cast their shadow over him for a time, but the Government in 1805 granted him a pension of £200 a year, and his affairs became thus more relieved. But then he was plunged in despair, and his whole future life was darkened, by the death of his little son, Alison. For weeks he was incapable of mental work, and although his latest volume, *Gertrude of Wyoming*, published just before his bereavement, was hailed with delight, Campbell was unmoved by the flattery of press and critics from Lord Byron to the penny-a-liner, and he never throughout his life recovered from the blow.

And now another domestic calamity was to afflict him. His only surviving son developed some malady which made him incapable of doing anything for himself; his studies came to an abrupt close, and soon Campbell was overwhelmed in bitter disappointment and sorrow. Even so, the poet—wisely, too—was working to full capacity. As editor of the *New Monthly*, and in his other literary and poetic work, his time would appear to have been fully occupied; but amongst it all he contrived to bring into being what he personally claimed as " the only important event in his life's little history." This was none other than the founding of the University of London—a lasting monument to his name had he never achieved anything else in his life

Glasgow now honoured her eminent son. In 1826 he was appointed Lord Rector of his old University. Two years later the honour was renewed for a further term, without one vote being cast against him. For a third term he allowed his name to go forward, and this time his opponent was Sir Walter Scott. If a measure of Campbell's esteem and position is required, then, as already stated, the fact that he was re-elected against such powerful opposition is of itself sufficient. In the midst of this triumph Mrs. Campbell died and left the poet virtually alone in the world.

But the years were passing. When, in 1842, his volume, *The Pilgrim of Glencoe*, appeared, although the minor pieces were acclaimed as genius, the title-piece did nothing to enhance his reputation, and the fact that old age was coming upon him made him realise that his best days were past. The following year he decided to revisit the Continent. In July, accompanied by his niece, he set out for Boulogne and settled in a quiet hotel, later taking up permanent residence in the town.

It was now evident to his friends that there was something amiss with the poet's health.    In May he was confined to bed, and, notwithstanding all human aid—his old friend, Dr. Beattie, even travelled from England to exercise his skill—on June 15 the poet died in a foreign land at the age of sixty-seven.    If he did not live to complete the allotted span, he had a busy and a fruitful life, and he has left as his monument some of the finest verse in the English language.    The death of his little boy, followed by that of his wife, and his only other child's helplessness in an asylum, darkened his closing years and chilled his heart and outlook, but he did not live in vain ;  and after his death the great and eminent, from Peel downwards, vied in paying tribute to his memory.

I like to think of Thomas Campbell as the little Glasgow laddie who played pranks in the old High Street, and as the man whose mind was gentle and kindly, filled with sweet, wholesome thoughts—one who died as he had lived, loved by his friends, honoured for his genius ;  a man of character but yet without a serious enemy in the world ; and an honour to St. Mungo and the city of his birth.

**TIBBIE PAGAN.**
An Imaginative Portrait.

# ISOBEL PAGAN

## A Burns Contemporary

THE looms of time have woven many strange characters, but none more unusual than that of Tibbie Pagan. Even the annals of the eighteenth century, a period notable for its strange and unusual personalities, would be hard put to it to produce just such another. Of course, such a woman, living such a life, could not exist to-day. The social and moral outlook has altered : the once isolated lowland village of Tibbie's time is now within easy reach of the travelling public ; the law is more alive and penetrating and does not allow such types to flourish uncurbed. All that, be it said, is for the good of the community, but it does not detract from the interest which surrounds such quaint and unusual characters.

Most villages, at any rate, most villages in the western district of Scotland, had at least one bohemian, rhyming character. Men and women stand out more distinctly, were more natural, or rather less trammelled by convention, at that stage in the country's social development, when hard drinking was the rule rather than the exception, and when even the unco' guid numbered many hypocrites within its canting circle.

Study the inner history of any small township, and sooner or later there will turn up some Saunders Tait or Tibbie Pagan to get us wondering at the times and manners.

Muirkirk, the stage of Tibbie Pagan's weird life and cantrips, was no exception. The very name has a lonely sound—the kirk-in-the-muir or the muir-kirk of Kyle ; indeed, it is self-explanatory to those even who care nothing about etymology. And yet Muirkirk has seen its stirring times and is not altogether unknown in the writing of our country's story.

Not far from the township, on a lonely stretch of moorland, stands a monument erected to Richard Cameron and those who died with him at Airdsmoss. Old Cairntable has looked down on the moors and mosslands since time began in Scotland, but never on a blacker day than that. The information as to where the weary Covenanters lay was given by a neighbouring laird, who was duly handed his blood-money, and after his mansion house was burned a year or two later, his son and heir reminded him that it was perhaps an act of retribution for the deed which sent so many innocent men to their graves.

The Covenanting history of the district is a full one, as all who are interested in the subject know. However modern views and opinions may differ about their deeds, there can be no question that the Covenanters were strong, clean men, ready to lay down their lives for that best of all causes, individual freedom and liberty to follow the dictates of their own conscience.

That this austere outlook degenerated and "ran to seed" there can be little question. The pendulum in human affairs always swings backwards and forwards in sequence, and so we have those restless spirits, the product of such an environment, the Tibbie Pagans of this world.

Not that Tibbie Pagan was a native of Muirkirk, although she spent the greater part of her life there. Indeed, the true Muirkirk bard was John Lapraik, and if curiosity ever takes you to the moorland town, and you journey by way of Sorn and the breezy, upland road, down in a grassy dip you will espy a small monument erected to that poet by the members of the local Burns Club. Lapraik was an altogether different type, and although at one time imprisoned for debt, he was merely a victim—as were many other unfortunates—of the Ayr bank failure, an occurrence which ruined more than one family.

Occasionally a volume of Lapraik's work comes into the market, but Tibbie Pagan's book, published in 1805, is never mentioned, and it is improbable that a copy to-day exists, unless buried in some State collection. If Lapraik owes his place in letters to his association with Robert Burns, he was at least a minor poet and a man of considerable power, an altogether different type from our heroine.

New Cumnock parish can claim Isobel Pagan as a daughter, because she was born near Dalricket Mill in 1741 or 1742—authorities differ as to the exact year, and we need not particularise. From birth she suffered from a malformation in one of her feet, and she walked throughout her life with the aid of a crutch. Her nickname, self-bestowed, one which clung to her during her mature years, was "Pistol Foot," and it is self-explanatory. But her foot was not her only limitation. Poor Tibbie had a rather obvious squint in one of her eyes, and, moreover, suffered from a tumour in her side which affected any remaining grace to which she might have laid claim.

Tibbie Pagan thus cannot by any means be said to have been endowed with physical beauty, but mentally she was sharp and quick to a degree. Indeed, so bitter was her tongue, that most people feared to offend her, not knowing what she might say or what tales she might repeat ; and, be it mentioned, she was not afraid to strike out with her crutch, especially when in her cups. Yet, notwithstanding her physical deformities, her moral imperfections, she had a wide circle of friends, even admirers, and was noted for her singing voice.

But let Tibbie introduce herself—and even if *all* her faults are not encompassed in her verse, the lines will serve the double purpose of giving at least some account of her origin, and habits of life, and illustrating her poetic powers :

> I was born near four miles from Nith-head,
> Where fourteen years I got my bread ;
> My learning it can soon be told,
> Ten weeks when I was seven years old,
> With a good old religious wife
> Who lived a quiet and sober life ;
> Indeed, she took of me more pains,
> Than some does now of forty weans ;
> With my attention, and her skill,
> I read the Bible no that ill ;
> And when I grew a wee thought mair,
> I read when I had time to spare ;
> But a' the whole tract of my time,
> I found myself inclined to rhyme ;
> When I see merry company,
> I sing a song with mirth and glee,
> And sometimes I the whisky pree,
> But, 'deed it's best to let it be.
> A' my faults I will not tell,
> I scarcely ken them a' mysel' :
> I've come through various scenes of life,
> Yet never was a married wife.

There you have Tibbie—but not Tibbie at her best, or her name would have been forgotten with her own generation.

When Tibbie first took up residence in Muirkirk, she occupied a small cottage on the Muirsmill lands. This abode she deserted for a rather unusual hovel a mile or two from the town ; it was situated on the banks of the Garpel Water, consisted of a low arch, and had originally been built to serve as a brick-store in connection with Lord Dundonald's tar-works. The laird of that period was Admiral Keith Stewart, and he probably sympathised with the deformed, friendless woman. If so, his pity was vain, because rarely did an evening pass but the abode resounded with what someone has termed " licentious mirth."

Although she possessed no licence for the dispensing of drink, Tibbie always had a goodly supply on hand, and her house became the nightly howff of all who loved a glass and a song. The drinking was not confined to her customers, because the poetess joined in the potations, and her voice was always loudest in the rather indelicate choruses.

The busiest time of all was when the grouse shooting commenced in August. Tibbie, being notorious for her wit and sarcasm, the gentlemen who came to shoot on the moors did not consider their vacation complete without at least one evening spent in her kitchen, where they were highly entertained by the singing of her own songs and the bitter repartee which she exchanged.

By way of a change, Tibbie was sometimes invited to spend the evening with the shooting party, and on these occasions, on her way home, long after midnight, her pocket liberally supplied with money and her mind confused with the quantity of drink she had consumed, she invariably maintained a loud conversation with herself, calling down curses and imprecations on anyone who had offended her. Her fierce and ungoverned temper, and her readiness to use her crutch on any person who annoyed her, assured that she wended her homeward path unmolested.

As already mentioned, she had a remarkably fine voice, and was ready to perform at any time when curious visitors called or the social glass was going round. Her master-piece was a ballad called " The Humours of the Glen," of which her friends and customers never grew weary. Indeed, when her social hours so befuddled her that she had to be put to bed, she would sit propped up and sing it with gusto. On one occasion, a travelling party of entertainers visited the town of Ayr, and a number of gentlemen who attended the performance entered upon a bet with the manager of the theatre that they could produce a singer from the country who could outshine his leading vocalist. The bets were settled ; Tibbie was interviewed and willingly agreed to enter the contest, and she easily won the bets for her patrons.

Although, in every sense of the word, irreligious, Tibbie is said to have been able to recite the whole of the Bible, but that fact did nothing to inspire her with awe or reverence for the wearer of a black coat. There are several tales of her feuds or lampoons on the ministerial brethren of her time. One will suffice. Every reader of Burns is familiar with the " Holy Fairs " of the period. On such a Sabbath in Muirkirk, a well-known and highly-respected, if slightly hysterical, minister was officiating at the open-air sacrament, when Tibbie, attracted by the crowd, hirpled up on her crutches. Enquiring of one of the congregation what the minister was preaching about, she was informed that he was endeavouring to clear up " some points of faith." Standing full in front of the preacher, and fixing her bright, quizzical eyes upon him, she said in a loud voice, " You're *borin'* awa', I see ? "

Some of Tibbie Pagan's verses enter upon what Allan Cunningham terms the " borderland of impropriety," but she lived in a rough day ; indeed, included in her collection was a song by Boswell, the biographer of John-son, which was not very fit for polite ears. The times were uncouth, and in that respect our poetess was probably no worse than the lave. But Tibbie's reputation is not founded on any of her convivial pieces. Take down your Burns and look up the poem, " Ca' the Ewes "—not to be confused with " Ca' the Yowes," for you will find them both, the latter an improved edition of the other.

> Ca' the Yowes to the knowes,
> Ca' them where the heather grows,
> Ca' them where the burnie rows,
>> My bonnie dearie.

> As I gaed down the water side,
> There I met my shepherd lad ;
> He row'd me sweetly in his plaid
> An' he ca'd me his dearie.

And so on—five verses and the familiar refrain. There were originally six verses, but one has been deleted. Cunningham commented, "the last verse is very sweet and sincere." Here it is :

> While water wimples to the sea,
> While day blinks in the lift sae hie,
>> Till clay-cauld earth shall blin' my e'e,
>>> Ye shall be my dearie.

In his footnote in his *Songs of Scotland*, Allan Cunningham writes : " The song is partly old and partly new ; what is old is very old, what is new was written by a gentleman of the name of Pagan," which really goes to prove the slovenly manner in which our authority worked. The last verse, so admired by Cunningham, was written by Burns. The Ayrshire Bard wrote about it : " This song is in the true Scottish taste, yet I do not know that either air or words were ever in print before."

Burns was probably quite right in his remarks about the song never having appeared in print; indeed, he attributed it to the Border country. It was written by Isobel Pagan when in her thirty-seventh year, and became popular, as it well deserved to be.

Amongst the dross, some fine gold emanated from the old brick-store by Garpal's banks. Two songs, both of which were at one time popular, were " Jeanie and Me " and " The Crook and Plaid ; " these are Tibbie at her best, and merely prove what she might, in altered circumstances, have achieved. Here is the closing verse of " Jeanie and Me" :

> What though on her cheek
>   The red rose lose its hue,
> Her sense and good temper
>   Bloom all the year through.
> Time, swift as it flies,
>   Gives strength to her truth,
> And adds to her mind
>   What it steals from her youth.
>
> My Jeanie and me,
> My Jeanie and me,
> And who lives so happy
> As Jeanie and me ?

The other, " The Crook and Plaid," is better known— here is the opening verse :

> Ilka lassie has a laddie she lo'es aboon the rest,
> Ilka lassie has a laddie, if she like to confess't,
> That is dear unto her bosom whatever be his trade,
> But my love's aye the laddie that wears the crook and
>   plaid.

Poor Tibbie Pagan had parts above the ordinary run. Although she was well-connected, her people appear to have neglected her entirely and left her to be brought up by the old woman mentioned in her own verse. Her disabilities and odd appearance, together with an unhappy love affair in her younger days, embittered her outlook and soured her mind. Notwithstanding her dissolute life, she lived to see her eightieth year and died in November, 1821. Her fame, or notoriety, was such that people travelled from the surrounding towns and villages to be present at her funeral, and this notwithstanding the fact that the day was so wild and stormy that the cart conveying her remains could hardly make headway.

Tibbie was buried in Muirkirk, the home of her adoption. What a strange, lost creature she was—yet one who, with proper training and discipline, might have left us as her legacy some fine verse. The rich soil was there—but, alas ! it was choked with weeds.

# ALEXANDER SELKIRK

## The Prototype of Robinson Crusoe

THE man—or woman either, for that part of it—who cannot look back with a sense of pleasure to those youthful days when Robinson Crusoe was a real hero, a figure of glamour and romance, one to be envied for his adventurous life on a desert island, has missed something good in life. Daniel Defoe created a character never likely to fade from the breathless page of youthful reading —and it is good that it is so. A fine, clean book, ranking with *Tom Brown's Schooldays,* or those exciting adventures told so many years ago by Ballantine, Henty, or Jules Verne, stories which one likes to think still hold their own against the more neurotic productions of modern times.

The story of *Robinson Crusoe* must, of course, be treated as fiction, but even so there is an atmosphere about the book which makes the hero's adventures to be very real, and the proof lies in the fact that, once read, the narrative is never wholly forgotten ; and that fact alone is a wonderful tribute to the author.

The original of Robinson Crusoe, Alexander Selkirk or Selcraig, was a Largo man. The family name was really Selcraig, but Alexander changed his patronymic to Selkirk after he left Fife and embarked upon his colourful career.

He was the seventh son of his parents, born in the year 1676, and in those superstitious times the incidence of his birth served to tincture the general outlook with a vague superstition rather difficult to define if one is unfamiliar

with the social outlook. There is nothing in this " seventh
son " freit, but even to-day it has not quite lost its force,
meaningless as it is. Perhaps that seventh sonship is the
reason why young Selcraig was so much spoiled by his
mother. His father, John Selcraig, was a man of considerable substance who carried on a business as shoemaker
and tanner, the two crafts in his day being usually con-
joined.

Young Selcraig was a bright, active boy, usually
engaged upon some mischief or other, and, as his father was
a strict disciplinarian, the indulgent mother was constantly
framing excuses for her favourite, or concealing his pranks.
There was every excuse for a robust, imaginative boy
filling his mind with adventurous dreams and neglecting
the more sober things of life. Consider his environment.
At that period the East Coast was the merchant shipping
centre, and this was not infrequently a not too hidden term
for privateering. Scotland was an independent nation,
vieing for supremacy with her southern neighbour, England,
and not above taking full advantage of any weaker vessel
when a good cargo could be secured by the process of
scuttling the other craft. Just as Robert Burns owed no
inconsiderable portion of his imaginative faculties to the
tales recounted to him in his boyhood by an old woman,
so, too, would young Selcraig be regaled with the hair-
breadth escapes and adventures of Sir Andrew Wood, that
fine old Largo man who sailed the seas and whose name was
held in wholesome respect by the captains of more than one
maritime country. Tales to fire the imagination and arouse
a desire to follow in his wake.

The sailormen of Largo doubtless swapped many a
yarn about the doings of their fearless townsman, and the
boy would listen open-mouthed to countless strange tales.

G

He would learn how Wood served James III. on several occasions ; and of the adventures of Sir Andrew's two ships, the " Mayflower " and the " Yellow Caravel." How with these two craft Wood never hesitated to engage with the best of England, France or Portugal, until his fighting prowess made him an enemy to be feared.

In 1481 a squadron of English ships entered the Forth, and Sir Andrew, against heavy odds, attacked and repulsed the invaders.    Later in the same year we find him on the west coast, successfully defending Dumbarton against the English fleet.    If the reader wants more fully to know the atmosphere that must have filled young Selcraig's waking hours, let him read *The Yellow Frigate*, by James Grant. Nurtured on such fare, is it to be wondered at that a lad of spirit found himself at variance with his father's wishes that he should settle down and spend his days making shoes ? To go to sea and look at the world was the lad's wish, and so there was constant dissention in the home.    So dire became the trouble that John Selcraig threatened to dis- inherit the boy unless he decided to fall in with his views. On one occasion, when discussing the matter, he grew so angry that he publicly threw his staff at the lad, warning him in his peremptory manner that "a whip for the horse, a bridle for the ass, and a rod for the fool's back " applied to his son unless the latter altered his outlook.

It is a little difficult to paint exactly this home picture : customs and manners have so completely altered within the past two centuries.    The father's word was law in his own home circle, and the kirk had a prying eye, always keeking and interfering in all manner of affairs.    These factors, combined with his genuine attachment to his mother, restrained young Selcraig from taking the law into his own hands and running away to sea.    Ostensibly at least, he fell in with his father's wishes, and in a half-hearted manner set himself to master the leather business. But his wayward temperament was continually getting him into petty scrapes—more, be it said, the result of high spirits than of evil ways.

And then, considering his environment and the customs of the day, the inevitable came to pass. In August, 1695, Alexander, then a lad of eighteen years, was cited to appear before the session for " indecent conduct in church." There was little in it, probably a matter of deportment or a smile at the wrong moment : but there it was ! His father was an elder, a fact which perhaps made the offence seem more serious. Be that as it may, the youth did not want to face the tribunal of the kirk or to run the gauntlet of his father's wrath. He was cited on the Thursday, and when his name was called out in kirk on the Sabbath there was no appearance. He had taken the plunge and run off to join a ship. He disappeared completely for six years, and there is not much doubt that during that time he was with the buccaneers in the South Seas.

In 1701 he arrived home in Largo, but by now a robust, turbulent man. He was one, so far as we can read, liberal and free in speech and manner, but quick to take offence and reckless of consequences. In any case, he was responsible for more trouble with the kirk.

In the November of his homecoming, Alexander, along with his father (still an elder), his mother, his brother John, and his sister-in-law, were all cited to appear before the session on a charge of disorderly conduct. The trouble arose over a trifle, but it might have had a serious ending. It appears that Andrew Selcraig entered the house with a can of sea-water and placed it on the table. Alexander, following and finding the can, and taking its contents for fresh water, took a drink.   Andrew laughed at the mistake, and the quick-tempered Alexander struck him with his staff.   The father intervened, and then his brother John, having been sent for, ran to help quell the disturbance.   By this time Alexander was thoroughly roused, had doffed his coat, and was being forcibly restrained from going upstairs to get his pistol.

The kirk took a hand in the matter, and Alexander was publicly rebuked from the pulpit in presence of the congregation.   The affair blew over, and as ships were then laid up during the stormy weather, we find him, much against his inclinations, assisting his father in the tannery until the Spring.   With the return of better weather, Alexander decided to leave home again.

The trade of harassing the Spaniards was a recognised career.   Captain Dampier, already known for his prowess in that direction, was fitting out an expedition which was not to return until it had " collected " £600,000 from the Dons.   Two ships were being equipped, the " St. George " with 26 guns, under Dampier in person, and the " Fame," of like armament, under a Captain Pulling.   So that this privateering expedition might have official sanction, commissions were obtained from the English Admiralty authorising its personnel to proceed in warlike manner against French and Spanish ships and towns.   Several merchants sponsored the affair by providing vessels and stores, and the agreement was on such a co-partnership basis that the officers and crew got no pay other than their agreed-upon share of all booty captured.   Luckily for our story, thieves fall out, and Dampier and Pulling had a serious quarrel on the eve of sailing.   The latter set off in his ship, but he must have fallen in with a better man, because his vessel was never again seen.

Dampier, loath to set out unsupported, now arranged to join forces with the " Cinque Ports," and of this latter ship we find Alexander Selkirk rated as sailing-master. On September, 11th, 1703, the ships set out in quest of adventure, to find on arriving at Madeira that, owing to their delayed start, the Spanish bullion fleet had safely reached a home port, and that they had missed their prize. This was a sad blow to their hopes ; but, a council being held, it was decided not to give up the voyage, but rather to proceed towards the Spanish Main in the hope of falling in with some ships, or, failing that, of looting a Spanish settlement.

Dampier, who was in supreme command, appears to have been of a vacillating type of mind, quick at conceiving grandiose schemes but lacking in the character to carry them through. When the two buccaneers—for that is what in truth they were—arrived at La Granda, an uninhabited island claimed by Portugal, they lay for a few days to take in wood and fresh water, and there Captain Pickering, of the " Cinque Ports," died and was buried on shore. Stradling, the acting lieutenant, was appointed captain, and it is to this change that we owe the romance of *Robinson Crusoe*.

These were wild men—men of ungovernable passions and tempers, ready to fight on slight provocation, and without any real discipline on board ship. Dampier's crew quarrelled with his new first lieutenant, and there was bad blood between them, so much so that Stradling left the " St. George " in a temper. A council was again held, and, after bickering and arguing, it was at length decided to sail for the island of Juan Fernandez.

In February they reached the island, and according to custom, decided to refit their ship and take in fresh meat and water. Now a violent quarrel broke out between

Stradling and his men. Out of a crew of sixty, forty-two mutinied, took to the island, and refused to serve on the "Cinque Ports." Among them was Alexander Selkirk. They employed their time wandering about the island exploring and investigating. At length Dampier got the two sides reconciled and the mutineers returned to their ship. While the men were still dissatisfied and on the point of again quarrelling amongst themselves, another vessel was observed, and, true to type, the buccaneers set out after her, their private feuds forgotten in their anxiety to capture the stranger. She proved to be French, and the "St. George" made up with her as darkness fell. In the morning the ships engaged, but the Frenchman was well manned and armed. The two fought for seven hours with considerable loss on either side, but as the wind had dropped the "Cinque Ports" was unable to come to the assistance of her consort. A breeze sprang up, the Frenchman escaped, and thus the loss of life, and the material damage sustained, brought no return.

This was the first of many unfortunate affairs, due mostly to vacillation on the part of Dampier, until ultimately the two captains had such a serious quarrel that they decided to part company and each act on his own. The combined crews were allowed to choose their ship; then, the change over on the part of those who desired being completed, the "St. George" and the "Cinque Ports" separated.

Selkirk remained with his original ship, under Stradling, and soon these two were quarrelling and arguing until matters came to such a head that "Honest Selkirk," as one writer named him, decided that, come what might, he could no longer serve under his captain. Lack of provisions, the state of the hull, and internal dissention at length forced Stradling to make for some safe anchorage where he could refit, and so the " Cinque Ports " was headed once more for Juan Fernandez. A month was spent scraping and cleaning, laying in a supply of wood and so on. It was a month of disagreement and strife between Selkirk and Captain Stradling; so bitter was their relationship that the Largo man decided to leave the ship, preferring to take his chance on the lonely island rather than carry on at sea in such circumstances.

Just before the ship sailed, Selkirk was landed. His sea chest and all his personal effects were put on shore, and then Stradling, who had come with him in the small boat, ordered the men to pull for the ship. When the boat was shoved off and the men were dipping their oars, his true position broke upon Selkirk, who shouted to Stradling to return and take him off. But this the captain refused to do ; Selkirk had been landed at his own request, let him make the most of it—and so the man was marooned on an out-of-the-way island rarely approached by his countrymen, and if taken off by a Spaniard it would be to exchange his lot for a much worse fate.

It was October, 1704, Spring in those parts, and Selkirk was surrounded by natural beauty enough to charm the coldest. But the voluntary castaway had no eye for nature. For days, scarcely breaking his fast, he restlessly paced the sands, always hoping that his comrades would return. The thought of winter, the knowledge that his friends had gone and that he must shift for himself, awoke in him a sense of reality, and he set about building a hut and storing dried seal and goat-flesh against the days when such might become scarce. As to his life on the island, perhaps *Robinson Crusoe* gives as good a description as we require, although it is not by any means a mirror of Selkirk's days.

Fiction based on fact might describe the immortal pages.

Selkirk, amongst other belongings, had a copy of the Scriptures, and spent his spare time reading it. According to one Rogers, a captain who sailed the seas and wrote a book on his adventures, dealing amongst other episodes with Selcraig and his island experiences, that worthy informed him that " he was a better Christian while in his solitude than ever he was before, and feared he would ever be again."

Food gave the solitary no worry, as the island was plentifully stocked with goats. His trouble was clothes, but he dried goats skins in the sun, sewed them with thongs of hide (remember his early training), and for needle used a sharp nail taken from his sea chest. That he went bare-footed was no hardship to one who had run about the fields and shore of his native land, where boots were never worn by children. One day he found some iron hoops washed up on the beach, and from these he constructed knives and scrapers. For several years one of these implements, brought home when he was rescued, was exhibited in the " Golden Head " Coffee-house near Buckingham Gate in London.

While *Robinson Crusoe's* prototype was passing the years on his lonely island, self-imposed as his hardships were, the world was not standing still. The " Cinque Ports " had been captured by the Dons, and Stradling and his crew were prisoners, a worse fate than that which befell Selkirk.

Dampier, with the " St. George," had safely reached England, but not with the immense booty he had promised his merchant sponsors. Now the restless captain was fitting out another expedition to harry the seas and take toll from the French and Spaniards. Two heavily-armed ships, the

**Portrait : " R. CRUSOE, as describ'd."**

The frontispiece to the fourteenth edition of Defoe's Classic, published 1778.

"Duke" and the "Duchess," were got ready. The Bristol merchants who financed the adventure agreed to everything except that Dampier be placed in command. They wanted someone of sterner iron ere they would risk their money on the venture, so Captain Woods Rogers was appointed. Dampier was nominated Pilot for the South Seas, and with crews totalling 333 men and carrying 56 guns, the consorts set sail as buccaneers in August, 1708.

On the advice of Dampier, they steered for Juan Fernandez, and on the last day of January, 1709, the island was sighted. Selkirk saw the ships approaching, and from his experience recognising them as British, he was beset with fears lest they should alter their course and pass by without making the bay. At once he set about collecting brushwood to build a fire, and then rounded up and killed a number of his goats so as to have an ample supply of fresh meat ready for his rescuers. When night fell he set alight his fire and kept it blazing throughout the dark hours. This beacon caused great consternation aboard the ships, as the island was known to be uninhabited, and Rogers and his people came to the conclusion that some French or Spanish ships were in concealment and awaiting their approach.

But it was a case of fighting or of lacking the water of which there was now urgent need, so the two ships were cleared for action as they cautiously approached the island. No hostile craft being seen, a boat with an armed crew put off to ascertain the cause of the fire and find out if it was safe to land. Alexander Selkirk met them on the beach. An odd figure he cut in the eyes of his rescuers. His beard had not been trimmed for four years and four months; he was dressed in goatskin, and, unused to conversation, was uncertain in his choice of words. Captain Fry and

Dover, who had taken their places in the small boat, invited him to come on board, but on being told that Dampier was accompanying the expedition, and until assured that the erstwhile captain had no authority and did not command, Selkirk hesitated about trusting himself amongst his new-found friends.    When on board the " Duke," Dampier came forward and greeted him in a hearty manner, informing Rogers that Selkirk had been the best man on the " Cinque Ports," and on this recommendation he was at once engaged as mate.

And now Alexander Selkirk roved the seas with his new friends, attacking and looting French and Spanish ships, until the expedition's term was up and the vessel made for home.    Rescued in February, 1709, he reached London in October, 1711, having been absent from his native land for fully eight years, half of which period he had spent on the island.    The prizes secured by the two ships during their adventures after Selkirk joined amounted to £170,000.

Selkirk, by his adventures and experiences, created great interest in London.    Sir Richard Steel met him and made him the subject of an article in *The Englishman*, in which he described his appearance and extolled his mind. Captain Rogers wrote a description of his own experiences and dealt fully with Selkirk.    Captain Edward Cook, also, put his travels in print and coloured the Juan Fernandez adventure.    Selkirk's name appears in several other contemporary books and journals, and in this manner his case came under the eye of Defoe.

When given his share of the prize-money, Selkirk set off to visit his old home at Largo.    He arrived on a Sabbath morning in the early Spring of 1712, to find his family had all gone to church.    Impatient to meet them again, he followed.

All eyes were on the stranger, but even his own mother did not recognise her son. Alexander kept his gaze fixed on his mother's face, and gradually it dawned upon her that the stranger, elegantly dressed in gold-laced clothes, was her missing son. With a cry she rose from her seat and rushed to his side, unable to wait until the service was concluded. All the Selcraig family left their pews, and, proceeding to their father's house, they welcomed home the prodigal.

Used to a wider view of life, the buccaneer could not settle down in the narrow Fifeshire townlet. After some little time, spent in restless wanderings and fishing expeditions, Selkirk eloped with a young girl, Sophia Bruce, and they were married in London. So hurried was his departure that he left his chest and belongings behind, and never again returned to claim them.

A dozen years later—towards the end of 1724—a widow arrived at Largo to take possession of a house left to Alexander under his father's will. She was not the person with whom he had eloped, Sophia Bruce only surviving a year or two as Mrs. Selkirk. The claim was fully substantiated, and having received her property, she too disappeared back to London, and so the last link with the buccaneer was severed.

Alexander Selkirk died in 1723, aged forty-seven. At the date of his decease he was a lieutenant on H.M.S. "Weymouth." His name and associations are still very much alive in Largo, although—dare one make the statement?—but for Daniel Defoe he would long ere this have been forgotten and unknown.

Seventy years ago a tablet was erected on the island of Juan Fernandez with the following inscription: " In Memory of Alexander Selkirk, mariner, a native of Largo, in the County of Fife, Scotland, who lived in this island in complete solitude for four years and four months. He was landed from the ' Cinque Ports ' (galley) A.D. 1704 and was taken off in the ' Duke ' (privateer) on 12th February, 1709. He died, Lieutenant of H.M.S. ' Weymouth,' A.D. 1723, aged 47 years. This tablet is erected near ' Selkirk's look-out' by Commodore Powell and the officers of H.M.S. ' Topaz,' A.D. 1868." When seeking for someone to do the lettering on the tablet, a man offered his services ; indeed, he almost claimed the job as a right, because of the fact that he had erected a tablet to Captain Cook's memory on the Sandwich Islands !

As we know, Defoe made Selkirk's experiences the subject of a book which is never likely to be altogether forgotten, and so made the island solitary's name and fame universally known. But it was an imaginary picture. In truth, Alexander Selkirk appears to have been a precious rascal, with just enough sentiment to make him the more dangerous to society at large. A sea-rover, a privateer with a copy of the Scriptures in his chest, but one who doubtless joined in many a scene over which—could we picture them—it would be better to draw a veil.

> A brave heart ne'er shall want for aught,
>   While a ship can sail the sea;
> The Spaniards they have gold in store,
>   And a rover's life is free.

Many a time Selkirk would join in that old buccaneer's chorus, and while, perhaps, his life and outlook suited the times in which he lived, to-day he would be given a short shrift.

But *Robinson Crusoe* is a fine tale, delightful and entertaining. Long may it continue to charm its countless readers—and so let us leave it at that !

**NIEL GOW.**

The original Raeburn portrait now in the Scottish National
Portrait Gallery, and reproduced by permission of the Director.

# NIEL GOW

## Maestro of the Fiddle

THE Scots have always been a music-loving race. At one time, it is true, the stranglehold of the kirk instilled in us the superstition that anything not sombre and sad was a deadly sin, thus effectively transforming us into a race of hypocrites, our joys and gaieties to be dressed in hodden-greys. Niel Gow, Robert Burns and a few—too few—such great souls did much to dispel that nightmare, and not before time. Nothing in this world is so elevating, so inspiring, brings such surcease to weary hearts or kindles such light and laughter, as appropriate music. Not the jumble of high-class orchestration which so few healthy, normal people truly understand, but rather the simple ballad music with which Scotland as a nation is so richly endowed—the " auld Scots sangs," the reels and strath-speys, the simple music of the heart which lives as part of our everyday life.

There cannot be evil in such tunes. Yet once-upon-a-time, in a certain district, the Parish Kirk minister forced his parishioners to break up their fiddles because the playing of them was sinful! In less remote years the introduction of church organs was opposed in many quarters ; and even now, in some places, there is a feeling that praise which is led by instrumental music " gets nae higher than the roof." And yet *all* music, if produced in the proper spirit, is worship—worship of beauty, of tone, of everything fine and good and pure. Many years ago in a little upland village I knew a household where the father got his daughter to play " O a' the airts " on the piano every Sabbath just before he left for morning service.   He said it put him in tune with the Infinite.   As a country laddie I did not then really understand what he meant.   To-day I think I know.

Yes, music is one of the precious things in life, alive and vital, and, like the human character, the simpler it is the better.

The music of Niel Gow is of the simple kind—direct, forceful notes, notes that make the feet beat time, that dispel all thoughts other than the mere pleasure of the moment.   And that, too, is as it should be.   When something clever—outstanding enough to last and not be forgotten—is said about a man and his deeds, no matter what he may actually have achieved or created, that man has the cloak of the immortals draped over his arm if only his other qualities allow him to don it.

> Gow and Time are even now ;
> Gow beat time and Time beat Gow.

That's good enough to illustrate the point—albeit the name of the man it was written about is not likely to fade so long as there's a fiddler still alive !

Of course, the fame of the name Gow is not all invested in Niel.   Many claim Nathaniel as a greater musician, and that may be so on the deduction that a son who follows his father's craft or profession is born into an atmosphere conducive to his exertions, favourable to his studies, and with the added advantage of his sire's minatory counsellings.

Niel Gow was born at Inver on the outskirts of Dunkeld on March 22, 1727.   It was intended that the boy should follow the craft of plaid-weaving, but his musical propensities early developed and ere long he laid aside the shuttle to devote himself to the violin. In such times there were not many opportunities for help or tuition. True, he must have had examples to inspire and spur him in his art, because his native county of Perth was celebrated about this period for its performers on the violin, the favourite music being strathspeys and reels.

When about thirteen years of age the boy was no mean performer, but, being entirely self-taught, he must have lacked a certain technique. And then one John Cameron, no mean exponent, took him in hand, and his progress was accelerated.

So swift was his advance that before he had reached his majority, Niel Gow carried off first prize in an open competition. It appears strange to us, perhaps, to realise that this competition was held in 1745, and merely goes to show how little events even of the greatest national importance influence the immediate lives of people as a whole. Amongst those who took part were Gow's own tutor, John Cameron, and one James Dow, who later took his place as a skilled player and favourite composer. But even such exponents of the bow had to yield the place of honour to the young lad from Inver, because Niel Gow triumphed over all his competitors.

The judge was an old man, who, although a skilled musician, was blind. In awarding the prize, he remarked that he was never in doubt as to who was the finest player amongst those competing; indeed, he said he " could distinguish the stroke of Niel's bow amongst a hundred."

From that date Gow's progress was continuous. From having no rival in his own neighbourhood his powers developed until he was at the head of his profession in the entire land. His hold on the public was such that he was always in demand, and Niel and his fiddle became almost a part of the social life of the country, no gathering being a complete success unless he supplied the music.    Many other exponents before his time and since, sharing the lime-light and applause, lived and flourished and died, to be forgotten in a short time.    The name of Niel Gow is still green.

The appearance and personality of the man were in his favour.    Erect, well moulded, with a keen and fearless eye, Gow, in the years at any rate when he was known to a wide public, always dressed in tartan knee breeches, and was the possessor of a quaint and sometimes biting humour.    He was no fool, but, on the contrary, a shrewd, pawky man who knew his place in the social order and yet was possessed of sufficient character and self-respect to enable him to mix with the highest gentry in the land and remain self-assured and confident of himself.    All his long life—he survived for eighty years—he made his home at Inver, and was never tempted, even in the heyday of his fame, to leave the little cottage or to vie with others, or (the downfall of so many temperamental artists) to spend his money foolishly.

Many tales and incidents are related about the fiddler, a number of which throw an altogether wrong light on his character.    Hail-fellow he necessarily was, playing at social gatherings and balls where his duties for a time almost turned his night into day.    Indeed he was normally making for home, his violin under his arm, when the early-rising section of the people were preparing to commence their duties.    Remember, too, there were few abstainers in the eighteenth century, and such a glamorous figure as Niel Gow, with a word and a quirk for most, was not likely to escape the scandalmongers.    Yet in his own home, unless there were visitors, he seldom drank anything but water.

His ready wit in part clothed him with a reputation he was far from deserving.   On one such occasion he had been playing at a ball near the bridge of Almond, and was wending his way home, his fiddle, as usual, under his arm. Some friends meeting him as he started off on his walk to Inver condoled with him about the length of the road he had to travel.   " It's no' the length o' the road that's fashin' me—it's the *breadth* o't," replied Niel.   On another occasion, when he was relating some incident to a circle of friends, one of them interjected, " But I suppose you would be the worse of drink, Niel? "   "The waur o' drink," replied Gow, " na, na, I may have been fou' but I wisna the waur o't."

Stories of this nature, circulating around such a public character, were bound to spread and earn for him an ill-deserved reputation.

Niel was never forgetful of the main chance, and knew how to take advantage of every opportunity.   When in Edinburgh in 1793, playing at the Caledonian Hunt Ball, he decided to call, ere going home next morning, at the leading music-seller's in the city and purchase a new bow. The man in the charge of the shop was a little uncertain of the exact social, or rather financial status of his customer, and proposed a bow priced at half-a-crown.   The maestro indignantly waved it aside.   Next one was produced of a little better quality, but this, too, was refused.   " Surely you have something better than these ? " queried Gow " This one," replied the shopman, handing over a bow, " is the finest quality obtainable, but it costs twenty-five shillings."   " That's more like it," said Niel, " Now, give me some rosin and let me try it."   But to this request the music-seller refused to accede.   He did not allow a new bow to be rosined unless definitely to be purchased.   Taking up a violin, he handed it to the customer with the remark that as it had lately been played on it would serve his purpose. " What about some music ? " queried the violinist, casting his eye around the store. By this time the shopman was convinced that he was dealing with a bumptious amateur, so, selecting a sheet, he handed it to Gow, and in a rather sneering manner remarked that it was newly-published and that, as his customer could not be familiar with it, if he could play it over without mistakes, he could have the bow as a gift. It was a copy of a new piece, " Pease and Beans," composed by Niel Gow. Adjusting the strings, Niel treated the man to an exposition of violin-playing such as he had never before heard. When the performance was completed, he handed the bow to the shopman with the remark, " It will do. Tie it in a bit paper." and, taking up the new bow, he turned and marched out, leaving a wiser if rather crestfallen man to his own thoughts.

Living at Inver, Niel was naturally in close proximity to the noble house of Athole, and the duke and duchess took a great interest in his progress and allowed him many familiarities. Indeed, when the musician was sitting for his portrait by Henry Raeburn, the duke would accompany him and chat about music or any subject to keep Niel in good countenance. When the hour was up, they would leave the studio and walk off arm in arm, the duke and the cottar, all social ties forgotten in their friendly relationship. Sir Henry painted four portraits in all for wealthy admirers —a proof of Niel's standing and the appreciation of his contemporaries.

The Duchess of Gordon was another of Gow's admirers, and she, too, developed into a warm friend. Once when visiting him to have a chat she complained of a headache and giddiness, on which the outspoken Niel remarked,

" Faith, I ken something o' that, too, your Grace : when I've been fou' the nicht afore, I've a feeling as if a swarm o' bees were buzzin' in my bonnet."

One August morning, in 1787, Niel received a request to go to Dr. Stewart's house for breakfast, when he would meet Robert Burns. Without delay he obeyed the summons, and after the meal the fiddle was produced and the poet sat enraptured by the strains. When the piece, " Locherroch-side," was played, Burns admired it so much that he expressed a wish to have a copy so that he might write words to suit the music. The result was the " Address to a Woodlark."

Niel Gow was twice married, and by his first wife, Margaret Wiseman, he was blessed with a family of five sons and three daughters. His second wife also, Margaret Urquhart, predeceased him, but there was no family from the latter union. Of his sons, three: William, John and Andrew, gained reputations as violinists worthy of their paternal name, but Nathaniel, the youngest, was the son whose name is best known in musical circles.

When a boy of sixteen, Nathaniel, by his talents, became so widely known that he was appointed one of the royal trumpeters for Scotland, an honour he retained until his death. Not merely as a violinist did he contribute to the common weal, but—what was perhaps more important —he devoted much time to collecting and publishing his father's original compositions in addition to his own works. Nathaniel had a son, Niel, who unfortunately died while a young man, but not before showing considerable promise ; amongst others of his compositions he left us the beautiful melody, " Bonnie Prince Charlie."

To anyone not seriously interested in music, but nevertheless " fond of a tune," there is bound to be much confusion as to which Gow actually composed the piece being played. It could not be otherwise, because, and naturally, Nathaniel at the height of his fame and powers, played many of the airs created by his father, Niel.

Niel wrote the tune, " Wha'll be King but Charlie," but its spirited rendering by his son drew attention to it and at least helped to gain for it a share of its well-deserved popularity. When Nathaniel was playing at the Caledonian Hunt Ball in Edinburgh, in 1822, the function was graced by the presence of George IV., Nathaniel included " Wha'll be King but Charlie " in his repertoire, and so well did he render it that the King went over and asked the name of the tune. " Wha'll be King but Charlie," said Gow, with a bow to his king, to the no small embarrassment of the assembled guests within hearing. His Majesty requested Gow to play it over again, and on more than one subsequent occasion of a like nature ordered that this particular tune should be included in the programme.

One of Nathaniel's most popular compositions is " Caller Herrin'." The manuscript of the verses, written in a disguised hand, was given to him by a lady, a friend of the authoress, in the hope that it might sufficiently appeal to him to set the words to music. In the letter enclosing the verses to her friend, Lady Nairn writes : " If it be of any use to Nathaniel, perhaps it should be dedicated to the Duchess of Athole." Needless to say, Nathaniel Gow appreciated the worth of the verses, and his setting combined to make " Caller Herrin' " one of the most beautiful of our Scottish songs.

Niel Gow died on 1st March, 1807, in the eightieth year of his age. He had lived a busy and full life, and one not without its compensations, for he was ever a cheerful, humorous man, ready to make friends and willing to help his fellows. He was buried in Little Dunkeld church, where a memorial was erected to him by his two surviving sons, John and Nathaniel. John Gow acquired a fortune as a musician in London. Nathaniel was not so fortunate in his financial affairs. Although at one time in quite a good position, he latterly lost much of his savings. Nathaniel and his father Niel are the Gows referred to when the name is spoken in connection with Scottish music.

It is good to be able truthfully to say of a man that the world would have been a poorer place had he never lived. That statement may be bountifully made with reference to Niel Gow. A kind and indulgent husband and father— an honest man in his dealings with his fellows—Gow, by his contributions to the social enjoyment of our country, keeps his name fresh and green when many a greater is forgotten.

# TOBIAS SMOLLETT

## Man of Letters

THE name Smollett is not a very common one, and yet it is at least familiar to most. Even those who have been denied the pleasure of reading his books, know something about the author or are familiar in a vague way with something he has said or done. Personally I never pass Cameron House on the banks of Loch Lomond, or cross the Fruin water, but his name comes unbidden to my mind. Renton, Bonhill, Dumbarton—the very mention of the names awakens memories of the Scot, who, like so many other brave souls, fought a losing fight with the scythe and was cut down before he was ripe for the gleaning.

Tobias Smollett came of good stock. The Smollett family were esteemed as of considerable local rank for many generations, and occupied quite an important social position in the County of Dunbarton. Considering his lineage, Tobias could hardly fail to possess certain gifts or endowments, or, at the worst, to be blessed (or cursed) with that restless disposition which marks the man who achieves his aim if only for the reason that his adventurous spirit drives him on to the attempt. He was born at a period when feudalism was not yet extinct and when the clan system had not as yet been irretrievably broken on the bayonets at Culloden Moor. Moreover, his home was situated in a district where tartan feuds and forays were no uncommon events in the life of the community.

Smollett's grandfather married a daughter of Sir Aulay Macaulay of Ardincaple, a family whose exploits in the claymore days formed none too peaceful a chapter. Another of his ancestors took in marriage a daughter of Sir Patrick Houston of Houston, a well-known Renfrewshire family. If we could give literal credence to all that Tobias wrote, we could also throw light on a minor historical mystery by stating that it was one of his forbears who blew up the Spanish Armada ship " Florida " in Tobermory Bay in 1588.

Tobias George Smollett, to give him his full name, was born in the old house of Dalquharn in the parish of Cardross in 1721, on a spot near to the present township of Renton. In those days it was an altogether different environment. A quiet, sylvan retreat, with the river Leven flowing amidst fields and woodlands, the scene of his youthful days did much to cultivate his mental outlook as he roved amidst the beauties of a countryside still noted for its native charm. Ben Lomond, Ben More, and a hundred massive peaks stood out as a background ; while Dumbarton Castle, and probably in those days the falling walls of Cardross where The Bruce died, would enliven his mind and nurture tales of the long ago. The Colquhoun country, bordering the untamed domains of the Macfarlanes and MacGregors, lay at his door, with Sheriffmuir but an episode of yesterday, the '45 still to come. The topic of his elders, certainly the ambitions of his schoolfellows, would be of raids and reprisals, in which the doings of Rob Roy would not be overlooked.

Such, then, was the atmosphere into which he was ushered, and its influence can be marked in the fact that while still a lad at school he composed some verses on Wallace.

To-day the district has changed its character and the streets and houses of Renton occupy the Smollett domain. Even so, the family connection still lives in the fact that

Renton was a Mrs. Smollett's maiden name, and the rising town was christened in her honour.

To say that a Scot—above all others—reveres his native town or glen, and that, no matter where he may wander, whatever scenes he may witness, he mentally compares all alien places to their detriment with his beloved homeland, is a mere truism.   Smollett could give articulate expression to his thoughts, and in prose he tells us :—" I have seen the Lago di Gardi, Albano de Vico, Bolseno, and Geneva, and I prefer Lochlomondside to them all."   In verse, he sings a similar strain :—

> On Leven's banks, while free to rove,
> And tune the rural pipe of love,
> I envied not the happiest swain
> That ever trod the Arcadian plain.

The lad had the advantage of passing his schooldays under a really good teacher.   John Love, of Dumbarton, was a man of outstanding ability, and one devoted to his profession.   He wrote a number of books and pamphlets, and ultimately became headmaster of Edinburgh High School.

Young Smollett, fired with the tales of his neighbourhood, decided to embrace the Army as a profession, but his grandfather, a man of wide experience, thought he could better his career if he took up medicine, so the lad was transferred to the College of Glasgow.   In time he was articled as an apprentice to a Mr. Gordon, a man with a local reputation as a physician.   Later he introduced this Mr. Gordon into his work, *Roderick Random*, under the name of Potion.

At this period he was continuously writing satires and humorous verses on his elders, or at least on those whom

TOBIAS SMOLLETT.

he considered to be rather too pompous ; this he did to the delight of all his friends and acquaintances, heedless of the fact that such weapons are oftentimes inclined to be double-edged, and that the satires would not tend towards his personal advancement in life. But his time was not devoted entirely to study : indeed, he was a healthy, stirring youth, fond of fun and ready to take his part in any exploit.

It was a winter evening and the Glasgow streets were blanketed in snow. A snowball fight was in progress between students and apprentices ; one of the latter was the apprentice of that surgeon who was later to figure as Crab in *Roderick Random*. This lad had been left in charge of the surgery while his master went out to visit a patient. The fun had proved too appealing, and the youth had left his post to take part in the encounter, when in the interim his employer returned. When the apprentice ran back he was very severely taken to task for his breach of duty. By way of excuse, the lad told his employer that he was standing behind the counter making up prescriptions when someone threw a snowball from outside, and that he had merely rushed out after the delinquent. "A very probable story," was the retort. "Can you imagine any-one throwing a snowball at me from the street ? " As the doctor turned his head, to point his remarks by fixing his eyes severely on his assistant, he was suddenly struck on the face by a large snowball. Young Smollett had been stand-ing behind a door pillar, listening to the dialogue, and this was his manner of helping his friend.

About this time, Tobias suffered a heavy loss by the death of his grandfather, who had left him practically no provision for his future. His support withdrawn, he was now dependent upon his own exertions, and as a youth of nineteen, his apprenticeship finished, he migrated to London

in search of advancement.   Clever, of lively imagination,
well read, possessing a rich vein of humour, and withal of a
most prepossessing personality, the young man had every
prospect that fortune would smile upon one so equipped
to take his place in the wider sphere offered by the metropolis.
After many unsuccessful attempts to have a tragedy
accepted by some theatre managers, Smollett secured
a position as surgeon's mate in a naval vessel.   The work,
with its drudgery and discipline, failed to appeal, so, relin-
quishing his commission, he left the ship at Jamaica.
There he made the acquaintance of Anne Lascelles, a
young lady of great beauty and attraction, who ultimately
became his wife.

In 1746 he returned to London to find the cruelties of
Cumberland a topic of conversation amongst all classes of
the people.   Although he was a Whig, the savage excesses
stirred his feelings and swayed his mind towards the
Jacobite cause.   The result was his ode, *The Tears of
Scotland* :

> Mourn, hapless Caledonia, mourn,
> Thy banish'd peace, thy laurels torn.

When the original six stanzas were circulated,
Smollett's friends warned him to be careful, for, even if no
official action should be taken, such an outburst would not
help him in his profession.   As a result of the warning,
he added still another verse, more strongly expressing his
views :

> While the warm blood bedews my veins,
> And unimpair'd remembrance reigns,
> Resentment of my Country's fate,
> Within my filial breast shall beat.

In the same year he published some satirical verses entitled *Advice*, directed at the leading politicians and public men of the day. A few months later he issued a continuation or sequel, *Reproof*, which was an undisguised attack on military characters, army contractors, and other questionable notabilities of the hour. These productions were not calculated to make the author popular in official circles, but they certainly made him feared and respected as one who had the ability to express his thoughts in striking fashion, and a man of such fearless calibre as to be above pusillanimity or toadying to any one, no matter how influential or important.

Smollett now married Miss Lascelles, but her dowry, which it was hoped would enable the young couple to set up a suitable establishment, led to extended litigation, and resulted in the Smolletts losing the case, with its consequent fatal blow to their financial expectations.

Perhaps from one point of view it was as well that the case went adversely, because now Tobias had to settle down and make an effort to earn an income to provide a home. The result of his exertions was his novel, *Roderick Random*. The book proved an instant success, and brought the author a considerable measure of fame and fortune; its success prompted further effort, and *Regicide*, which followed, still further enlarged his reading public. When Tobias was only thirty years of age, in 1751, there followed *Peregrine Pickle*, a book rather coarse for the present taste, but perhaps suited to the age for which it was written.

Notwithstanding his literary success, Smollett was still desirous of following the medical profession. He was successful in obtaining the degree of Doctor of Physic, but, his efforts to establish a practice proving vain, he now decided to devote his full-time energies to literature. He retired to Chelsea, and in due time there was published another novel : *The Adventures of Ferdinand Count Fathom.* Some years had passed since the now successful author had left his native land, so he decided to pay a visit to his friends in Scotland. After residing for some time with his mother, who had by now removed to Peeblesshire, and renewing acquaintance with a number of friends, he returned to London to continue his literary career.

In 1756 he started the *Critical Review,* personally contributing voluminous articles, many of which were marred by his failing of intemperate language and satire. He fell foul of more than one literary man whose pen was dipped in gall; indeed one wonders, in times like our own, at the freedom of expression and invective then permitted, which would to-day result at once in legal proceedings.

Here are one or two short extracts to illustrate the point: if now highly humorous, they were originally penned in deadly earnest: "They appear to be physicians without practice, authors without learning, men without decency, and writers without judgment." In a reply to some criticism and defending Smollett from a previous attack, here is another and an abridged quotation :—" [one] whom he has reviled, bespattered and belied, with all the venom of low invidious malice, and all the filth of vulgar abuse." This from a serious review, written and produced for the benefit of cultured readers and political in its aims, is a pointer to the times. Certainly it would not be permitted to-day. It is worthy of the valiant Mr. Potts of the *Pickwick Papers* and his feuds with the rival contemporary. But this sort of thing could not go on indefinitely and unchecked. Smollett ran foul of a certain Admiral Knowles. Amongst other words he wrote that Knowles

" was an admiral without conduct, an engineer without knowledge, an officer without resolution, and a man without veracity." These were strong words, and they ended in Smollett being fined £100 and sent to prison for three months. While undergoing his sentence he was not idle, and passed the days in writing *The Adventures of Sir Launcelot Greaves*. This book proved popular only in respect of the author's reputation; it was bought and read because of his former works, but in itself it did little to enhance his reputation.

Next, turning his attention to more serious work, Smollett completed in 1764 a *University History* in forty-two volumes, while he also produced a *History of England from* 1748 *to* 1765. For each of these works he obtained substantial payment.

But now the author's state of health began to cause concern to his friends. While he was still a young man— little more than forty—his sedentary life and long hours at the desk began to exert their toll on even his strong constitution. The death of his only child, Elizabeth, in her fifteenth year, was a crowning blow, and he was prevailed upon to cease his labours for a time and take a well-earned rest. In June, 1763, he went abroad for change and relaxation, remaining away for two years. During this sojourn his health remained impaired to such an extent that his very outlook on life altered and he now took a jaundiced view of everything that crossed his path. It was not the real *Smollett* who wrote *Travel Through France and Italy*, but a nerve-tortured man altogether unlike his true self.

Sterne took him to task for his views, and in a rather splenetic passage wrote: " The learned Smelfungus travelled from Boulogne to Paris—from Paris to Rome— and so on : but he set out with the spleen and the jaundice,

and every object he passed by was discoloured and dis-
torted . . . ' I'll tell it,' said Smelfungus, ' to the world.'
' You had better tell it,' said I, ' to your physicians.' "
Smelfungus was, of course, Smollett, and more of the like
strain may be found, by those interested, in the *Sentimental
Journey*.

The foreign tour having failed to effect a cure, Smollett
decided to revisit his native Scotland in the hope that the
bracing climate and a renewal of old friendships would
combine to dispel his disorders. In 1766 he arrived in
Edinburgh, where his mother now resided, later proceeding
to Glasgow, and thence to Cameron House on the banks of
Loch Lomond, his cousin's home. This change failing
to renew his condition, he spent the winter in Bath, but
again without permanent results. His adventures and
experiences were, however, used for his last and—as most
admirers consider—his greatest work, *Humphrey Clinker*,
which was published in 1771. More than one leader in
Edinburgh society served as a model for the characters in
this novel. The Matthew Bramble of the book is a delinea-
tion of the author himself. But the years were not proving
kind to Smollett, and when the novel made its appearance
he was residing in a small cottage near Leghorn, his bodily
ailments having once more driven him abroad in search of a
cure.

But, home or abroad, there was to be no cure for
Tobias Smollett. On 21st October, 1774, his sufferings
came to an end by his death at the age of fifty-one.

So passed one of the outstanding figures of his time,
a name for ever engraved on the annals of Scottish letters.
A monument, in the form of a column, was erected to
Smollett's memory at Bonhill, not far from the place of his
birth. This memorial was financed by his cousin, while

the inscription is the united effort of Dr. Samuel Johnson, Professor Stuart of Edinburgh, and Mr. Ramsay of Ochtertyre. Although he had earned considerable sums, Smollett left his widow in what can truly be termed necessitous circumstances. Had he survived for another year, he would have fallen heir to Bonhill and a substantial private income, but his death deprived the widow of any rights under the entail.

Mrs. Smollett (the Narcissa of *Roderick Random*) was now practically stranded in a foreign land, without funds or experience of managing affairs. Her husband's estate, it is true, was left to her, under trustees—one of of whom was Mr. Graham of Gartmore—but the amount was too insignificant to lend such assurance or security to one trained and bred as she had been, and her position was now serious. Smollett had been too independent in his views, had indeed too often dipped his quill in vinegar, to encourage the hope of help from those in authority in London. Mr. Graham—for he, it is presumed, was the prime mover—exerted his influence, and procured for the widow a benefit performance at the Theatre Royal in Edinburgh. This took place on March 3, 1784, when the play produced was *Venice Preserved*. A prologue was written for the occasion by Mr. Graham. The result enabled a sum of £366 to be remitted to the widow in Italy.

# CAPTAIN BARCLAY

## A Great Pedestrian

WE live in the day of the open-air cult. Never at any time have field sports and games claimed so many devotees, occupied so much space in the newspaper columns. But many have discovered the truth that not in games or sports is the best of life's leisure to be found, but rather in tramping the hillpath and drove road, exploring the byways. The love of nature, the wonder of flower and bird and beast, is a trait that grows and develops mind and body, and is not to be thoroughly appraised or enjoyed in the pages of books.

But the nature lover, the true rambler, is not akin to the hiker, whose only ambition is to cover so many miles per day without deviation to enjoy a vista or a leisurely halt or to listen to a bird.

Of course, I have nothing against the hiker ; good luck to him or her ; but sometimes these toilers leave me slightly bewildered. Go where you will of a week-end, even in the short winter days, be the path ever so secluded, the track ever so remote, it will be a wonder if you do not meet some hiker bowed under a heavy rucksack. Sometimes I inwardly wonder of what these huge loads consist. On one occasion I walked from my Scottish home to North Wales, my only encumbrance a light haversack and a light waterproof ; and even now, with the tramp a mere memory, I am glad it was not then fashionable to carry a heavy pack, or I, too, might have fallen a victim to the craze, with resultant memories of fatigue and hard going. Still, the movement is all to the good, and better the open road with a heavy

pack than loafing at home, and so, long may it continue !
It is developing a new type, breeding an independence, a
robust and sane outlook upon life which was unknown in
great measure to city dwellers in the more artificial environment of the Victorian days.

Byways and hillpaths where but a few years ago the
bleat of a sheep or the whir of a grouse alone broke the
silence, are certain to have their quota of youths and girls,
sturdy and tanned, who are there not because of fashion but
because they really like the exercise and freedom from
people and pavements. Last summer, when walking up
Glen Doll and across the high wind-swept heather-track
to Loch Muick, I met more walkers in a couple of hours
than one would expect to see in like time in a village street.

Hugh Walpole said something to the effect that the
battle never ceases, only the battlefield alters, and so it is
with walking. To-day that exercise is optional, because
never at any time in history were there provided such
facilities for travelling by train, 'bus or car ; whereas a
generation ago, apart from a certain social caste, it was a case
of walk or stay at home.

Many great men—men who achieved fame and
celebrity by their imaginative work—were open-air walkers.
When Thomas Carlyle left his home to study at Edinburgh University, he tramped the sixty-odd miles. George
Borrow thought little of walking from Norwich to London,
R. L. Stevenson has left us a record of his countryside
peregrinations. Charles Dickens, until circumstances inter-
vened, always walked some six miles after breakfast. One
could go on multiplying instances and examples at length,
but even amongst the best of them their prowess would
fade before the feats of Captain Barclay.

It is of course true that modern training methods have

I

speeded up walking as an athletic event where competitors stripped and spiked, compete on a cinder track. Such men as J. W. Raby, who walked three miles in some twenty minutes and five miles in thirty-five minutes; or G Cummings' mile in six minutes twenty-two seconds, have made pedestrian history, but these are record-breaking events by specially trained professionals. There is no comparison between their feats of the arena and the distances covered by Barclay, a country gentleman, on turnpike roads, such as they were in his time.

As a lad of fifteen years his walking exploits were becoming known, and for a private bet of one hundred guineas, he wagered that he could cover six miles of the Croydon road within the hour. The attempt was made in August, 1796, and Barclay won. Two years later, and again under a sweltering sun, he won a walking match against a London clerk known for his feats of distance and endurance. The starting point was Fenchurch Street in the city, and the course was to the tenth milestone beyond Windsor. Barclay accomplished the distance, seventy miles in fourteen hours, and won comfortably. Four months later, in December, when every condition might be expected to retard his progress, Barclay again left Fenchurch Street and walked to Birmingham by way of Cambridge. The distance, one hundred and fifty miles, was completed in two days. After resting for a day or two, he walked back to his starting point, but altering his route by way of Oxford, in like time.

Captain Barclay was born in 1779 and came of well-known Kincardineshire stock, the Barclays of Ury, men of which family were noted for their strength and stamina. Young Barclay was sent to school in England when a boy of eight years, and later was at Cambridge. His military

CAPTAIN BARCLAY.

title arises from the fact that in 1805 he was gazetted to the 23rd Regiment. He was robust above most men, of assured position, and spending much of his time amongst the officer class; it naturally followed that his physical gifts were developed, and in a gambling age, with ample means at his disposal, many of his feats were performed as the result of wagers.

He did not, however, invariably win. On two occasions he lost his bets to a Mr. Fletcher of Ballingshoe by failing to accomplish ninety miles within twenty-one hours. But so confident was he of his power that for a third time, for a wager of five thousand guineas, he backed himself to perform the distance in November, 1801. With such a large sum of money, and in great measure with his reputation as a pedestrian at stake, Captain Barclay entered into his preparations in a serious manner. He engaged as his trainer an old farmer connected with Lord Faulconberg's estate, a man noted for his own walking abilities, and on whose experience and judgment he felt he could rely. The wager, as already stated, was to be decided in November; and in October Barclay had a full-dress try-out.

He walked one hundred and ten miles in nineteen hours and twenty-seven minutes. This was good going, more especially as it was raining heavily all that day. The arena was Lord Faulconberg's park, and the conditions were such that he was at times ankle-deep in mud.

The actual date of the wager was to be fixed by giving eight days' notice, and now that he was in top form it was considered wise to fix it without delay. November 10 was chosen, and the track upon which the attempt was to be made was a measured mile on the road which ran from York to Hull. Barclay had to cover the distance ninety times within twenty-one hours or forfeit his five thousand guineas. One fact lost sight of was that he must encircle the post set up to mark the distance, and that entailed additional walking, true, only a pace or so, but it was an extra handicap. Lamps were placed by the roadside so that the walker could choose his steps and keep to the line when darkness fell, a necessary precaution on a public turnpike in the month of November. Time-keepers were stationed to see that everything was done to ensure fair play to both sides. The walk was dated to take place on a Tuesday, and a few minutes before midnight on the Monday evening, Captain Barclay, accompanied by a number of friends and supporters, arrived at the starting post. Mr. Fletcher, with whom the bet was laid, was also present.

At midnight precisely, six stop-watches were set and placed in a box, which was then sealed and given into safe custody at the winning post. Immediately the watches were set, Captain Barclay started off on his arduous task. He went at a steady, controlled pace, and for the first sixteen miles averaged something like thirteen minutes per mile. At this stage he left the road and entered a house, mutually agreed upon, for the purpose of taking some refreshment, and another handicap, of course, self-imposed, lay in the fact that by so doing he had to walk an extra twenty-odd yards. At this halt, as at every subsequent refreshment interval, he completely changed his clothing. Another fifteen miles was covered, then once more refreshment and entire change of apparel.

By eleven o'clock forenoon Barclay had walked fifty miles and was still fresh and vigorous. And so it went on, until he had accomplished the full distance, which he did at twenty-two minutes four seconds past eight o'clock on Tuesday evening. The official time made him winner by one hour seven minutes and fifty-six seconds within the limit set down. He could easily have gone another twenty miles without evincing distress, but when he completed the last lap the spectators rushed forward and carried him shoulder-high to his dressing room.

The following summer, in August, 1802, Barclay displayed his exhaustless stamina by walking from his home in Ury to Kirkmichael, most of the way leading him by rugged mountain paths. He remained at Kirkmichael for a day and a night, without, however, going to bed, and then walked home again; but as he returned by Crathynaird the detour added another twenty miles to the journey, so that, without sleep, he tramped one hundred and eighty miles !

Although remembered for his pedestrian feats, Captain Barclay was also a noted runner. In June of 1803 he took on a match to run against Burke, the pugilist, who was known for his speed. This event he won with ease. At a later date he was matched against another known athlete, John Ward, this trial to be one of a quarter mile, where speed throughout was a necessary qualification. Barclay finished in the lead, his time being exactly fifty-six seconds. At Eastbourne he ran two miles, the wager being that he could not accomplish the distance in twelve minutes. He again won in good style, with two and a half seconds in hand.

A Captain Marston, of the Forty-Eighth Regiment, himself a well-known pedestrian, now challenged Barclay to run a mile for a bet of one hundred guineas. This was a severe test, and the match attracted much public interest. The two officers were known for their heel-and-toe prowess, and many bets were made on the outcome of the meeting. The day of the race was intensely hot, yet Barclay once again triumphed, doing the mile in five minutes and seven seconds. That race was responsible for another challenge, this time the stakes being five hundred guineas. Barclay's opponent was a Manchester athlete, John Ireland, and known for his fine running powers. The distance was one mile, and the Captain made the pace so hot that Ireland gave up without completing the course.

But a repetition of the many bets and wagers won by this remarkable walker would become tedious. He met and defeated, one after another, the best men of his day, be they sporting amateurs or noted professionals, and always for substantial sums laid as wagers. On most occasions when he was competing, so great was his fame and reputation, crowds of spectators turned up on horse-back or on foot, and many bets were offered and taken, with the odds generally against Barclay's opponent. These must have been colourful meetings, and sometimes I think the atmosphere of Barclay's contests might almost be found in the chapters of *Rodney Stone*, although I cannot think of a Corinthian amongst that sporting company who had the Captain's stamina and staying powers.

An example of his wonderful endurance, even though not quite authenticated, is almost sufficient to cast doubt on his record. It is, of course, true that he performed the ordeal—for that is the only word I can think of to classify his performance, although he himself did not appear to consider it anything extraordinary—and few people, even the most robust, would care to repeat the feat.

In August, 1808, Barclay was the guest of Colonel Murray Farquharson, of Allanmore, in Aberdeenshire. At five o'clock in the morning he started for the grouse moor, and it is known that he walked at least thirty miles that day amongst heather and rough ground. At five o'clock he was back at Allanmore, and after partaking of some refreshment he started out to walk to his own house at Ury, a distance of sixty miles. He had no halt on this journey, and accomplished it in eleven hours. There were a number of affairs calling for his personal attention, and to these he devoted himself without taking any rest. He was fully employed until the late afternoon, when he set out for Laurencekirk, sixteen miles away, where he attended a ball. He danced all night, and then walked home to Ury, where he arrived at seven o'clock.

That would be more than enough for most men, but Captain Barclay was cast in more heroic mould. Instead of resting, on being told that partridges were in the vicinity, he went after them, and spent the day in shooting. Just consider the performance : two days' shooting over heavy going ; an all-night dance ; at least one hundred and thirty miles walking, three days and two nights without rest, indeed strenuously employed, and you have the measure of this extraordinarily vital man.

The outstanding performance of the Captain's career, and one for which his memory still remains green in the minds of those interested in athletic events, followed his wager with a Mr. Wedderburn Webster, entered into in October, 1808. The ordeal—for that again is a just term—was to commence on June 1 of the following year, and Barclay was to walk one thousand miles in one thousand successive hours. Note the terms, because that was the crux of the whole affair. He could not do two or three miles and then rest for a period— the wager was one mile per hour for one thousand hours. Several noted athletes had already failed in this event, and even his own friends were doubtful of Barclay being able to stand the strain of such a prolonged exertion without proper intervals of rest. Few of those who attempted such a trial and who persisted in carrying on when it was obvious they could not complete the course, escaped without more or less serious injury to their feet or legs. Another adverse factor was the serious wasting; for instance, one well-known athlete lost over three stones in weight in twenty-three days, and had to give up from sheer exhaustion. The mental and physical strain, combined with lack of sleep and regular recuperative rest, simply made the task a seemingly impossible one even for the most robust.

When Barclay started off in his heroic attempt it was a warm June morning. The stage was the public road at Newmarket, and was not altogether ideal for the purpose. As the days passed the crowds grew denser, until the workmen had to rope off the ground, otherwise his supporters and admirers would have crowded him so much that progress would have been impossible. There was not a bed to be had in Newmarket, Cambridge, or any town or village within many miles of the scene, and every horse and coach within a wide radius was hired on the owner's terms.

It would be tedious to follow the diary of this herculean exhibition, although everything was carefully logged, even to his meals and duration of sleep. On the forty-second day, at three o'clock in the afternoon, the last mile was completed and Captain Barclay had made pedestrian history. It is perhaps worth noting that he did the first mile in twelve minutes in rainy, close weather, and took exactly twenty-two minutes to complete the last lap under a hot sun. His time gradually declined from the first week, which averaged 14 minutes 12 seconds, until the sixth and final week when he required 21 minutes 4 seconds.

He lost fully two stones in weight during the period. Within a week of winning his bet he had joined Lieut.-Gen. the Marquis of Huntly as aide-de-camp and was on his way to active service in the Walcheren expedition.

It is perhaps worth mention that Barclay, when engaged upon one of his walking matches, shuffled rather than walked as we understand the term. He did not raise his feet more than two or three inches from the ground, and thus conserved every ounce of energy. He took a remarkably short step, bending slightly forward and throwing his weight on to his knees.

Of course, apart from his walking powers, any man who could perform as he did required to be of exceptional physique. Barclay was not a particularly heavy man ; he weighed something over thirteen stones, but he was exceptionally strong and well developed. On one occasion (with a straight arm) he threw a half-hundredweight twenty-four feet, and then, lifting it, he tossed it over his head a distance of fifteen feet. How that compares with modern records, I do not know, but it is sufficient to prove the point. On another occasion, when the officers of his regiment were in the mess-room, Barclay allowed a Captain Keith, the paymaster of the Company, to stand on his right hand ; then, steadying himself with his left, he gradually raised himself and deposited the officer on the dining-table. Captain Keith weighed eighteen stones, so the feat took powerful muscles !

Notwithstanding his many wagers, his physical prowess and high social position, Captain Barclay was no spoiled or affected braggart. He was a plain, one might with truth claim, a cultured, country gentleman, with a sincere respect for the rights of others : a man held in affectionate esteem by his tenants, with a large circle of friends, free and generous in his outlook on life and ever ready to help those in distress.

When considering his feats and performances, we must remember that they are hardly comparable with like attempts to-day, with scientific training methods and prepared arenas. Captain Barclay rarely, if ever, trained for any of his events, most of which arose out of sporting bets made amongst his friends in a caste of society which has very much altered under our more prosaic mode of life.

# THE WARLOCK LAIRD OF FAIL

IF you, reader, live in the west of Scotland, you will probably know the old, ruined walls of Fail, a place so pressed by the hand of time that it promises soon to be nothing but a memory. The passing centuries have dealt harshly with the ancient pile, and now only a section of wall stands gaunt and grim, with that rather pathetic look about it which all neglected, aged things don when their day of usefulness is past and there appears to be no place for them in a busy, hurrying world.

Fail Castle—or rather all that is now left of it—stands in a romantic corner of Ayrshire. It is surrounded by memorials and steeped in memories of days long gone by, of enthralling interest, or matters of little moment, according to one's outlook on life.

Often I go to Ayr by car, but always by the " back " road. It leads by Loudoun Castle and then through the village of Galston, both places ripe with tales of other times. As the road climbs up, I pause at the summit, beside a cluster of ancient beech trees. From my view-point, the Castle—the Windsor of Scotland, as someone has justly termed it—lies far below in its wide parkland, the old tree under which the Treaty of Union was signed, more than two hundred years ago, still keeping ward over the mere saplings of a century. Loudoun Hill stands out, a dominant feature, and between stretch the " bonnie woods and braes " of Tannahill's undying song. To one who knows his Scotland, the vista gives birth to many memories of the country's story—of Wallace, Burns, the wild fighting

Kennedies, to mention but a few at random.   Then on again until the Kilmarnock-Mauchline road is behind, round the little haugh, across the Cessnock water at the point where once there was only a ford, and then the dark firs are passed which enfold Carnell.

Another mile or two, and towering high amidst its bower of trees stands the Burnweil Monument, the traditional site from which Wallace and his patriot band gazed upon their work in the burning Barns of Ayr.   Not far off, but hidden by grassy undulations, lies Craigie Castle, or rather all that is left of its once massive walls, as if brooding upon the tales and legends of far-off days, and almost forgotten deeds, of which it is the centre piece.

Again the road takes a bend, and on the left, as if perched upon a hill-top, the spire of Tarbolton Kirk pierces the heavens, lifting its pinnacle far above the clustering houses.   There in a field, just by the roadside and directly opposite the little cottage and workshop where apparently farmers' carts are constantly under repair, you will see a broken, gaunt skeleton, grey with age and tottering towards a final eclipse.   You are looking at Fail, the one-time home of the Warlock Laird.

A romantic figure he was, if ever there was one : so, let us select him for one of our studies.   Admittedly by so doing, we leave the realm of known facts and descend to mere mythology, or, at best, romantic lore.   There was indeed such a person, but so many queer tales have been woven round his name that it is impossible—at least for the writer—at this late day to sift the grain from the chaff, to dilate with certainty upon the actual personality of the man.   As we know, the walls of his house still stand, but only just.   One day a sou'-western gale will blow over all that remains, and then, perhaps, without the visible proof that such a place actually existed, the spectral shadow of the weird owner also will disappear from public ken and be for all time forgotten. That, at least, is the fate of more than one old keep and its warlike owners, whose names mattered for a generation or two and then faded, leaving only a halting verse or mutilated tradition to prove that they actually existed.

Fail was not always a castle. Indeed, it was originally built as a monastery, the Monastery of Fail. It housed a community known as the Red Friars, and the now tottering walls were founded as far back in history as the year 1252, so that it has seen many changes in its time. The monks of those days—in Scotland, at any rate—do not appear to have been of the austere order one instinctively associates with their title. Certainly the fabled monks of Fail were not so; they savoured more of the sybarite than of the anchorite, if one can believe the old verse associated with their exploits. But they must have been jolly, lusty fellows, fond of good cheer, and yet withal as good men as some that followed at a later date and who dared not smile lest they committed a cardinal sin.

The Fail monks were garbed in a white habit, embellished with a red and blue cross upon the shoulder, quite a conspicuous apparel, as you will admit, and so mayhap if one of them did " gang a kennin' wrang " his garment would serve to show him up like a beacon on a dark night. This defence of the order is necessary if justice is to reign, because the verse, the only fragment I can trace about the old monks, is rather sore upon them.

> The Friars of Fail
> Get never ower hard eggs, or ower thin kale ;
> For they made their eggs thin wi' butter,
> And their kale thick wi' bread.

There is no great indictment in that, you say.    No, but have patience, here is the real crux of the matter :

> And the Friars of Fail they made gude kale,
> On Fridays when they fasted ;
> And they never wanted gear enough
> As lang as their neighbour's lasted.

Well, wherever they got their eggs and kale, it certainly lasted, because the monastery stood and flourished for fully three hundred years. It stood in good times and in bad until Fail went the way of all, or nearly all, the monasteries at the Reformation.

When the monks were cleared out, the lands and buildings—as so often happened—were annexed by the man with the longest sword. After passing from one family to another, Fail and its rights and perquisites were granted in 1619 to one Walter Whyteford, a grant ratified by the Scottish Parliament two years later. The Craigie family would seem to have had some prior claim, but apparently it was set aside in favour of Whyteford. This Whyteford we are entitled to assume as the actual Warlock Laird, although now we are dependent upon ancient lore rather than indisputed fact.

The new master of Fail had lived abroad for some years, probably educated in France, and, as many contemporary Scotsmen were, he was for some time a wanderer upon the Continent. In any case, he often uttered strange and meaningless words to his servants and tenants. He was, moreover, rather outlandish in his dress and behaviour, and was decked with a long flowing beard. Please remember he flourished at a time when witchcraft was rife ; and he must have been a man of considerable influence and standing, or one who instilled great fear into the hearts of his neighbours, or he would undoubtedly have finished his career at the stake.

His abode alone was enough to mark him as unusual. The cells formerly occupied by the monks surrounded the superior's house in which the laird took up his abode, altogether an unchancy, eerie place in which to live. But the Warlock Laird did not care a bodle. His was the power to make cows withhold their milk, to filch butter from the churn, to bewitch people and make them answer to his will. But even these things were mere trifles with the Laird, the frills of the profession, as it were ; his reputation is founded upon feats of legerdemain much more sinister than such old wives' tricks. In a word, he had the evil eye, and the whole countryside went in terror of him.

One point must be made in his favour : most of his astounding cantrips were of a humorous nature, and he never wantonly used his uncanny powers to take human life or seriously harm his neighbours if they left him alone. He was, I think, a little vain of his powers, and liked to mystify his company by an exhibition of them. But sometimes, although not often, he was worsted by even greater forces than those in his employ.

The Laird had company, and in an idle moment, when standing at a window which overlooked a wide expanse of agricultural land, one of his guests pointed out that no less than twenty ploughs were visible, preparing the ground for the coming harvest season. This was the type of occasion in which the Laird revelled. Turning towards his assembled guests, he offered to take on a bet that by repeating a certain magical formula he could bring every plough to a stand and that they could not proceed until he removed his spell. The wagers were laid, the Laird recited his magic words, and on the instant eighteen out of the twenty teams stood stock still as if petrified. Two went on ploughing, unaffected by the magician's powers. At once enquiries were set afoot, and it was discovered that the two in question had parts of their framework made from wood of the rowan. As the whole world knows, rowan-trees dispel charms and evil-workers, and thus the Laird was frustrated and lost his bet.

This failure did not, of course, affect his prestige, because it was quite understood that not even the Warlock Laird could prevail against a sprig of rowan. There is an old couplet or saying which sums up the position :

> Rowan-tree and red thread
> Make the witches tyne their speed.

Chambers tells of an old medicine-man living near Loch Awe, who as a charm or specific against witches and supernatural beings sold sprigs of rowan, along with certain prescriptions, to the people in his district. So great was the demand that he left a considerable fortune to his son, and he made such good use of his heritage that the son in turn became a landed proprietor. Many a witch and warlock has been frustrated, and their fell designs brought to nought, because of a rowan lintel on a door !

But it is not for me to make excuses for any failure on the part of the Warlock Laird. He was more successful on another occasion. A travelling packman, with a little cart drawn by a donkey and loaded with the coarse china dishes and crockery so dear to the heart of the country housewife, happened to pass the castle gates. The Laird, who was taking the air with a friend, at once offered to bet that he could make the pedlar smash all his stock, piece

by piece. The bet was accepted, and to the astonishment of
the other, the packman halted his cart and commenced to
dash his china on the ground, nor did he desist until the
ruin of his load was complete. On asking the now ruined
man why he had acted in such an absurd way, he was
informed by the pedlar that a black dog or other fierce
animal thrust its head out of each dish in turn and girned
and growled at him. He was so afraid of what it might
do if left amongst his china that he smashed the pieces up
in the hope that as each was dashed to the ground he might
dislodge the unwelcome intruder.

To me that appears rather a cruel misuse by the Laird
of his mystic powers, unless—and tradition is silent on the
point—the magician compensated the unlucky pedlar for
the loss which must otherwise have plunged him into
penury.

One of the Laird's cantrips, more amusing in its
sequel, was seized upon by Joseph Train, who turned it
into verse and gave it to the world under the title of *The
Warlock Laird of Fail*. The tale goes that one fine morning
the Laird, in company with his friend and neighbour the
Knight of Craigie, were engaged in the chase. What they
were hunting is not revealed, and so I cannot enlighten you
on the point. Perhaps they were coursing hares, because
there were no rabbits in any part of Ayrshire in those days ;
but the quarry is unimportant. In the course of their sport,
they chanced to come upon a farm-house where the good-
wife was busy brewing ale for the shearers and the extra
men engaged at that season.

The chase had been long and arduous, and the enticing
aroma of the ale induced Sir Hugh, the laird of Craigie,
to dismount and ask if they might have a cog of the new
ale. The old lady was more than honoured to entertain

K

her laird, but she expressed fear and horror at the very sight of the Warlock Laird and refused even to let him cross her door.

Craigie laughed at her fears, and pointed out that he, too, had a long beard, and might also be taken for a warlock, but she was adamant and refused to permit his friend to enter the house, or indeed to have anything to do with him. She frankly told Sir Hugh that the Warlock Laird had already been responsible for the mysterious death of her best milch-cow; moreover, he had bewitched her bairn; coupet her kirn on many occasions, and had also cast a spell on her dog, which as a result had died. Sir Hugh could make nothing of her, so he rejoined the Warlock Laird and explained the old lady's fears. Instead of sympathising with her very natural terror, he requested the magician to provide some sport by giving an exhibition of his powers.

"If you want sport," replied the Laird, "I wat ye's no want it lang." With this cryptic remark, he produced a " merry pin " from his pocket, and inserted it in the lintel of the door. At once the old lady dropped her task and began to dance and sing.

The Laird now called to the farmer to cease his work for a moment and fetch him a drink of ale. Whenever that worthy man crossed the threshold on his kindly errand, he, too, came under the spell and commenced dancing. The shearers now came home for their mid-day kale, and one by one as they entered the house, they, also, started to dance and sing like madmen. It was a warm day and as, per custom, the fire was situated in the centre of the floor, and each man was holding his fellow by the coat-tail, they danced round the fire, and although exhausted, they could not stop until the Warlock Laird withdrew the " merry-pin." When he ultimately did so, the whole company fell prostrate on the floor.

But the laird, for all his weird powers, was not immortal. When the day came that he knew he had not long to survive, he warned his servants not to remain in the castle after his death, and furthermore impressed upon his neighbours not to bury him until their harvests were safely gathered. He was most emphatic about the fact that his interment would be followed by a fearful storm.

When he died the harvest was just begun. The weather was ideal, the sun hot, and after a day or two, when the crops were half finished, it was decided to bury the laird. His last exhortation, now that he was dead and gone, was forgotten by many and scoffed at by others. But the laird's uncanny power was still working, although its author was no more. The moment the body was carried out there was a resounding crash—the roof of Fail Castle had fallen in as predicted. The morning had been bright and sunny, ideal harvest weather, but now the wind began to rise. Shortly it reached gale force, and then torrential rain flooded the harvest fields and destroyed the crops. Even in death, the Warlock Laird had vindicated his powers.

That is why Fail is an unchancy place of a dark night. If you do go to inspect the old ruin, choose a day and hour when the sun is bright and the motor traffic is thrang on the nearby road.

To anyone interested in witches and the horrible deeds committed by the professional " witch-finders," the name of Maggie Osborne will be familiar. This notorious woman, by means of her black art, could bring about storms at sea and drown innocent mariners, of course for a consideration paid by those who were likely to benefit by the act.    But the kirk got its talons into her at last.    She made a full and free confession of her misdeeds, helped thereto by being made to dance on a hot iron plate, as was the custom.    Of course, she was condemned to the stake, but even when the flames were crackling about her, such was her mystic power that she started to rise as if wafted by some invisible influence, and would soon have been free of her tormentors but for the quick-witted town officer, who, seizing his halbert, hooked the witch by her petticoats and drew her back into the pyre.

If you wonder at the introduction of a notorious Ayr witch into this short account of the Warlock Laird, let me explain.    Maggie Osborne was a natural daughter of the Warlock Laird, and—quite a new theory—perhaps it was she, watching over the remains of her father, who brought down the roof of Fail and destroyed the harvest on that ill-fated occasion.    In any case, it is an additional warning to leave the fell place alone—'tis an uncanny neighbourhood.

# JOHN SNELL

## Benefactor of Youth

IF you have not already enjoyed that pleasure, you must travel some day the circular route from Girvan to Ballantrae, and then, leaving the salt waters of the Clyde, keep company with the Stinchar as it flows by Colmonell and Daljarrock, and so back to your starting point. Every mile is clothed in beauty and steeped in romance.

For the first part of your journey the road winds by the rocky coastline and above ranges the Byne Hill, so beloved by summer holiday-makers ; then come Fell Hill, Grey Hill and Pinbain Hill, and you are fairly launched upon your adventure, and he is a poor creature who is not compelled to stop from time to time and enjoy the scene ere passing on in quest of further charms. You will pass at least six ancient strongholds, each bearing a name familiar in Carrick feud and foray. Memories of The Bruce, Peden the Prophet, the fighting Kennedies, and Robert Burns will continually stir your imagination. R. L. Stevenson tramped the long miles and found inspiration. Smugglers and their brandy-holes, witches, not to mention mermaids, and the horrible Sawny Bean, have left their traces. Many of these characters are alive to-day, because the pen of S. R. Crockett made them quick again.

Kennedy's pass has been reaped by time, and compared with a few years ago it is merely a name ; but old Ailsa Craig is one of the immortals, and there are few vantage points in the round where you will fail to find his massive head peering at you as if guarding the domain against

incomers.  Where he cannot follow, Knockdolian, the
" fause craig " of the seaman, keeps watch in his stead.
You will pass Gamesloup, where fair May Collean made
an end of her Bluebeard husband, the Fause Sir John, as
recounted in the old ballad :

> Fause Sir John a wooing came,
>   To a maid of beauty rare,
> May Collean was this lady's name,
>   Her father's only heir.

Sir John amassed a fortune by espousing wealthy ladies
and then throwing them into the sea at Gamesloup, not
far removed from his legendary home.  But he met his
match in May Collean, who put an end to his fell work
by pushing him off the rocks and calmly watching him
endure himself the fate he so richly deserved but had intended to mete out to his bride.

When Ballantrae is reached, you will leave what an
old writer termed " the great road to Ireland " behind
you, not without a mental tribute, as you pass, to the gaunt
walls of Ardstinchar, and then the valley of the Stinchar
will enfold you in its quiet beauty.  By a winding, verdant
road you will come to Colmonell, a village which many
far-travelled people term the most beautiful in Scotland.
It is a hardy claim, but one I should not wholeheartedly
dispute.  Certainly the setting is perfect, and if you
journey there in the proper season, the wild hyacinths will
be tinting the roadsides for miles until the whole place
seems unreal, and as if an atmosphere of fairyland had
enfolded you.

When Colmonell is a mile or two behind, you will
round a bend in the roadway, and there, on a little mound,

stands an odd-looking memorial. If you made proper use
of your opportunities in the village you would have visited
the little kirk, and you would not fail to note the gravestone
placed there in memory of Andrew Snell, who died in
March, 1663. The stone (since that date, of course,
renewed and preserved) was placed on the grave by instructions of John Snell in memory of his parents. If interested,
or indeed normally observant, you would share my surprise
at the lack of reference to his mother, although she, too,
sleeps there, but the reason for the omission is mere conjecture. The little monument by the roadside was in
turn erected in honourable memory of John Snell, and never
was posthumous mention more richly deserved. The
inscription is his biography in essence :

> Near this spot in 1629 was born John Snell, son of
> Andrew Snell, Smith in Almont. Scholar, Soldier,
> Lawyer, he rose by diligence and prudence to high office
> in the State, being Seal-bearer to King Charles II. He
> died at Oxford in 1679. To his memory this monument
> was by public subscription erected in 1915.

Although definitely stated as 1629, the exact year of his
birth is, I think, conjectural. We may accept it, and
perhaps not be far wrong, but in any case the fact is not
really material for our purpose. The only reliable authority known to me throws no light on the matter beyond
stating that no Parish or Session records were kept at that
period—an almost criminal neglect, but one in which this
parish did not sin alone.

If the year of John Snell's birth is a little doubtful,
his childhood and youthful days are equally obscure.
Doubtless, he was a normal, stirring country laddie, who

ran about the braes and fished in the Stinchar, but one must accept that on trust. His father was blacksmith for the district, and so must have been a man of good physique, and the natural inference is that the boy was healthy and robust.

The Stinchar valley, quiet and retired as it is to-day, would in the early years of the seventeenth century be bleak and wild to a degree. There were no hedges or dykes in all Carrick at that time, and no roads as we now understand the term. Mere hill-tracks or the paths beaten by the armed Kennedies in their passing to or from Craigneil or Ardstinchar. Even then young Snell would be safe enough in his play hours. There were not merely no motor cars speeding by his home, there was not so much as a horse-drawn carriage, while armed men looked from their vantage posts from more than one warlike peel and held watch and ward over all those who lived under the protection of their overlord.

That carries us back to a Scotland difficult to picture, at least, as viewed by a peasant boy. Warriors and churchmen, witches and Covenanters, we can dilate upon with fair knowledge and security, but with the bairn John Snell it would be wiser, and infinitely safer, to leave him undisturbed at his play. As he had two sisters, he would not want for company, and probably his life did not materially differ much from that of young Colmonell of our time.

And so, when next we meet him, it is the year 1643, and John Snell has passed his years of thoughtless romping, and is now a student at Glasgow College. Andrew, his blacksmith father, was probably a good craftsman and a bien man ; certainly he was ambitious for his only son, and determined to give him every chance in life.

When the Civil War broke out, Snell, then a youth of fifteen years, relinquished his studies and enrolled on the Royalist side. Here again we cannot follow his adventures other than in the knowledge that he took part in the battle of Worcester in 1651. That battle proved fatal to the King's men, and our youthful warrior had to seek refuge with some friendly partisans in the South.

Again the curtain is rung down over his movements, but when the young Royalist emerges he is obviously on the high road to fortune. Somehow and somewhere he becomes a protégé of Sir Orlando Bridgman, at one time solicitor and adviser to the king, and who has now, owing to the national outlook, which ebbed his fortunes, set up in practice in London. John Snell has obtained the position as clerk to this distinguished practitioner.

Then came the Restoration, bringing favour and advancement to many who had suffered for the cause, including Sir Orlando, who was now appointed Lord Chief Baron to the Exchequer. Young Snell was given a minor position in the court. Further honours came to Snell's patron until ultimately, by uprising steps, he attained the office of Keeper of the Great Seal. Snell rose in concert, and was now promoted a Seal Bearer, a position of trust and importance. But the favour of kings and courts is a proverbially fickle thing, and Sir Orlando was deprived of his office in 1672. He was succeeded by the Earl of Shaftesbury, but Snell, now a tried and trustworthy man, was retained in his position. He had other interests also ; indeed he must have proved a keen and energetic man of affairs, and judged by the standards of his time he amassed a considerable fortune.

If Snell's life was a full one, it did not stretch the allotted span ; he died in August, 1679, in the fiftieth year of his age. He set an example by the legacies he willed to his servants and dependants, and so disposed his affairs that his widow and daughter were plentifully endowed.

But the name of John Snell is not perpetuated by whatever good deeds he may have performed towards his contemporaries. Were that his only claim to remembrance, his name would long ago have been erased from human memory. No graduate of a Scottish University, no one interested in education in its wider aspects, but knows of the Snell bequest and what it has done for many young Scotsmen. Indeed, no calendar of Scottish names is complete which fails to include John Snell, and the only regrettable thing about the man is that we—or at least the writer—can glean so little about his personal life and habits. More than once the terms of his legacy have been the subject of litigation between the University authorities of Glasgow and Oxford, but the court has clearly defined the procedure to be followed, and to-day all is peace and amity. As to whether he ever returned to spend some time renewing acquaintance with the district of his birth, research offers no guide. Probably he did not, and that fact may perhaps afford a clue to the omission of his mother's name from the gravestone, a local craftsman merely carrying out the work according to his grasp of the written instructions. This, however, is mere conjecture.

In Snell's day there was not much to tempt anyone to sojourn in the valley of the Stinchar. After the softer pleasures of the South, where law and order and a certain measure of civilisation—not to say of culture—was taking deeper root among the people, a Scottish parish where such strongholds as Carleton, Craigneil, Kirkhill, Pinwherry, and Knockdolian (with a near neighbour in Ardstinchar) were ready at any time to prove their power was not a territory likely to be over-attractive to anyone whose avocations were performed in a more law-abiding atmosphere.

A mere clachan of thatched cottages in the eighteenth century, Colmonell would be even less enticing in the seventeenth. Times have changed, and, writing exactly one hundred years ago (in 1838), the Rev. Thomas Blair, then minister of the parish, congratulated his flock on one noted improvement in their social habits. Here are his words : " A greater degree of decency is observed at funerals, and the service which, in some instances, in olden times amounted to fourteen rounds of spirits and wine, has been reduced to three." Ballantrae was notorious for its smugglers, and brandy was cheap and plentiful, with its natural repercussion on all neighbouring villages.

It is to-day almost inconceivable, when motoring or tramping the Carrick coast, to picture the lawless stage of the district when the powerful Kennedy family held their station as above the law. We cannot blame John Snell for spending most of his days in the South amongst courts and dignitaries, and when he came to lay down his earthly task and account in person to the Highest Court of all, the charge could not be held against him that he forgot the land which gave him birth—and that factor would be given due weight in the final verdict.

# WILLIAM CREECH

## Burns' Edinburgh Publisher

FACING me on my bookshelves as I write is one of my most cherished possessions—the first Edinburgh edition of Burns' poems. Flanking it stands what is only, alas! a facsimile copy of the more valuable Kilmarnock edition. Since these thin volumes first appeared, a veritable library has been written around the poet. Every phase of his life, every action, has been probed and dissected until it would almost appear that the last word has been said! and then still another analytical work is published!

Sometimes when I raise my eyes and see the two—landmarks of Scottish literature, I term them—I let my thoughts rove for a little among the host of mixed personalities imprisoned within their covers. The saints and sinners, rogues and honest lads and lasses who are to-day so well-known to thousands of readers in every quarter of the world. It is a remarkable symbol of the bard's power, and forces one to ponder on life! There is hardly a personality in all the gallery—and they are all taken from life portraits, not fanciful sketches—but would long ere now have been forgotten and unnamed had not their path through life brought these men and women into contact with an Ayrshire ploughman. Take them away from the reflected light of the poet, and they become mere husks of yesterday, lost in the shadows of time.

And then I take the Edinburgh edition from off the shelf and once again examine it. Mint new it looks, fresh and clean as on the day it was issued from the press of

William Creech. A tribute, surely, to its value, to the protective care of former owners.

There is a short dedication by the author "To the Noblemen and Gentlemen of the Caledonian Hunt." It is addressed to "My Lords and Gentlemen," but it is not a servile page. It is a manly piece of writing in which Burns tells his subscribers that while he is indebted to them for their goodness, he "does not present this address with the venal soul of a servile author ; I was bred to the Plough, and am independent." It is signed Robert Burns and dated at Edinburgh, April 4, 1787. Then follows the list of subscribers in alphabetical form, occupying another thirty-eight pages. Quite a number (apart from the Caledonian Hunt, which took a hundred) ordered more than one copy. The list makes interesting reading, and one name in particular attracts the eye because of the fact that against it is the number 500—the name of William Creech.

Do publishers get sufficient credit for their courage in publishing the works of unknown authors—at best a speculative business ? Without the publisher, the author is like a coach without horses, potential but incomplete. William Creech it was who published amongst other notable volumes the Edinburgh Burns, and in more than one sense are we to-day indebted to his foresight and enterprise. Indeed he is another figure in our gallery who lived in, and personally helped to create, the "Golden Age" of Edinburgh's literary fame. Even allowing for his position, his enterprise, his municipal life, more important his culture and outlook, his name would long ago have disappeared from public ken but for one act. A few bibliophiles would be on nodding acquaintance ; students of old Edinburgh might come across traces of his activities in various business and social circles, and that is about all. The fact that Creech published the Edinburgh edition of Burns' poems has assured him of an undying name.

Strange was the almost Midas touch of this Ayrshire poet. Men and women who considered themselves as infinitely superior beings unwittingly became notables for all time because of his friendship. Village lads and dairymaids, whose counterparts to-day live and labour and die unknown, crossed the poet's path—and their names live for ever, to be known and remembered when statesmen and princes, scholars and professors are as forgotten as the clothes they wore. The Midas touch, indeed—transmuting common clay into the gold of immortality.

To such figures we may, in very truth, compare William Creech. His literary coteries, the wit and repartee which enlivened his bookseller's shop of an afternoon when the leading lights of the capital met, are, with a few notable exceptions, forgotten and unmourned. A young ploughman of some twenty-seven years visited the city—and his reflected light still glows undiminished on those who crossed his path or excited his interest, and amongst the number is the subject of our chapter, William Creech. The Edinburgh man was not even the first to publish the poems. Everyone is familiar with the name of John Wilson, although he must not be confused with the " Wee Johnnie " about whom Burns, dipping his pen in vinegar, wrote :—

> Whoe'er thou art, oh reader, know
> That death has murder'd Johnnie !
> And here his body lies fu' low—
> For saul he ne'er had ony.

The publisher was an enterprising business man, held in respect and esteem by his fellow townsmen. Along

**WILLIAM CREECH.**

An Engraving from the portrait by Sir Henry Raeburn.

with his brother, Peter, he founded the *Ayr Advertiser*, and on Peter's death John assumed as a partner the Rev. Hamilton Paul, a minor poet and a man who had it in him to achieve a higher rung in the ladder of life than he ever attained. But for " Wee Johnnie," William Creech and the Edinburgh triumphs of the poet might never have been staged. These, however, are mere musings and lead nowhere ; the reader may not even agree, so we will leave it at that !

William Creech was born at Newbattle, near Edinburgh, on April 21, 1745. That was a fateful year for Edinburgh and for Scotland generally, and witnessed the birth of another and greater figure, later to dominate the city and lead his fellows : Henry MacKenzie. Both men were destined to play important parts in the fate of the as yet unborn Robert Burns. Both came into the world too late to witness the ongoings in the city as a result of the '45, when the plain-stanes of the Old High Street echoed to the skirl of the pipes as the Prince marched in to hold camp and court.

Creech was a son of the manse. His father was minister of Newbattle. Within a month or two of the child's birth, the Rev. Mr. Creech died at the comparatively early age of forty, leaving a young widow (who, by the way, came of fine Devonshire stock), the boy, William, and two little girls—a great responsibility at any time, but the more so because of the unsettled state of the country, now in the turmoil of a civil war. Neither of the girls reached maturity, indeed, both died a year or so later, in 1749.

Following upon the death of her husband, Mrs. Creech had perforce to leave the manse, and she took up residence in Dalkeith. When the two little girls died, she removed to

Perth, probably anxious to get away for a time from an environment so charged with sorrowful memories. There young Creech was enrolled as a scholar, but we have no record of his progress. But early ties and sacred memories were calling, and the widow again returned to Dalkeith, and now William's education was given serious attention. One of the leading dominies of his time, a Mr. Barclay, was chosen for the lad, who was fortunate in having such a guide and mentor, and equally fortunate in the type of scholar with whom he was now associated. Such was the example, so deep the impression, infused by their teacher, that an association of former pupils—self-termed Barclay's Scholars—was formed and met once a year to renew old days and scholastic exploits. Most of Mr. Barclay's pupils made good in after life, and amongst those taking an active part in the social reunions were Lord Viscount Melville and Lord Chancellor Loughborough.

Mrs. Creech was left in anything but affluent circumstances, and so was forced to keep boarders to eke out her income. This was another fortunate circumstance for the boy, since it brought him into close personal contact with the Rev. Dr. Robertson, later minister at Kilmarnock. The Doctor was acting as private tutor for the sons of the Earl of Glencairn, and, taking an interest in young Creech, he devoted time and patience to aiding and guiding him in his studies. And more, a close friendship sprang up between Creech and the sons of the great Ayrshire nobleman, ties that were to last throughout his lifetime.

When her son was ready to continue his studies at the University, Mrs. Creech removed to Edinburgh. There she was shown much kindness by one of the leading families in the city, the Kincaids. Mr. Kincaid was a bookseller and publisher, a successful business man, who ultimately became Lord Provost. William Creech was at this time studying to enter the medical profession, but when one day Mr. Kincaid approached his mother with an offer to take him into his business as an apprentice, the prospect opened up was too tempting to refuse. When, in 1764, Mrs. Creech died, Mr. Kincaid took the orphan lad into the shelter of his own home and treated him as a son.

Anxious to progress in his career, Creech, like so many Scots before his time and since, went to London in 1766 to gain further experience, and from there he went to reside in Paris for a short period before returning to Edinburgh to settle down finally in life. By this time Mr. Kincaid had been appointed King's printer, was devoting much of his time to magisterial duties, and was becoming daily more immersed in public affairs. The result was that in 1773 he withdrew from commercial activity and handed over the business to William Creech.

For over forty years Creech the bookseller was a well-known and highly respected citizen, numbering among his friends many of the leading figures of his time. He was polished in manner and for the period widely travelled, having accompanied Lord Kilmaurs, the son and heir of the Earl of Glencairn, on his " grand tour " of Europe. In a former chapter in this series (Henry MacKenzie, The Man of Feeling,) we have already made reference to two Edinburgh publications, the *Mirror* and the *Lounger*, publications of a weight and position which it is difficult at this time fully to appreciate. Both were printed and and published by Creech, and they did much to bring him into closer relationship with the cultured and literary caste for which Edinburgh was then noted. He was the original publisher also of the works of Dr. Beattie, Dr. Blair, Dr.

L

George Campbell, Henry MacKenzie, Dougald Stewart
Dr. Adam Ferguson, Lord Woodhouselee and many others,
and though most of these names mean little to-day, they
point to men who were famous figures and intellectual
leaders amongst their contemporaries. But Creech did
not devote all his energies to business, successful as his
ventures proved. He served two periods as a magistrate,
and was for three years (1811-13) Lord Provost of the city.
But his municipal affairs, if they tended towards a busy,
useful existence, naturally did little towards the cultivation
of his literary and cultural life. Happily he received a
liberal education, read widely, and was something of a
classical scholar, and while a keen and enterprising business
man, his life was so ordered that he had many hours to
spare for social relaxation and that type of literary conversation then indulged in by men of a certain mental equip-
ment, but of which we to-day merely hear an occasional
echo. His morning room was the centre of attraction for
prominent men of all denominations from University
professors, church dignitaries, eminent writers and philo-
sophers, and public figures, and was known for a number of
years as " Creech's levee."

In one particular—indeed almost in a duty to his
fellows—Creech failed. A man in his unique position,
numbering amongst his best friends and acquaintances
all the outstanding personalities of what may without
exaggeration be termed the leading literary centre of Europe,
failed by neglecting to keep a written journal for the benefit
of later generations. His conversation glowed with refer-
ences to famous persons, with personal anecdotes of those
who had achieved fame in more than one walk in life. He
was an indefatigable correspondent, and his business as
a publisher brought him into close relationship with many

about whose lives and habits we would to-day welcome
more information.    On several occasions the suggestion
of compiling such a journal was made to him by friends,
and undoubtedly Creech intended to prepare such a work ;
but alas ! he kept postponing his task until it was too late.

Of Burns lore alone, William Creech had it in his power
to enrich our store immeasurably.    The two men were on
terms of the greatest intimacy, and such occasional
glimpses of their friendship as we come across in the works
of Lockhart, Allan Cunningham, and the rest, merely whet
our appetite and set us longing for more.

When, in May of 1787, Creech left Edinburgh for a
prolonged stay in London, Robert Burns was on his Border
tour.    On hearing that his friend had departed for the
South, the poet sent him a letter from Selkirk, dated May
13, which commenced : " My Honored Friend, The
enclosed I have just wrote, nearly extempore, in a solitary
Inn in Selkirk, after a miserable wet day's riding," and so
on.    The enclosure was his " Epistle to William Creech."
It extended to twelve verses, and gives an additional light
upon " Creech's levee," already mentioned :

> Nae mair we see his levee door,
> Philosophers and poets pour,
> And toothy critics by the score
>           In bloody raw !
> The adjutant o' a' the core,
>           Willie's awa' !

> Now worthy Gregory's Latin face,
> Tytler's and Greenfield's modest grace ;
> Mackenzie, Stewart, sic a brace
>           As Rome ne'er saw :
> They a' maun meet some ither place,
>           Willie's awa' !

The names mentioned were all outstanding figures in the Edinburgh of that time. " Gregory " was Dr. James Gregory ; Tytler of Woodhouselee ; Greenfield was Professor of Rhetoric in the University ; Mackenzie was the cultured Henry Mackenzie, " The Man of Feeling " ; and Stewart was Professor Dougald Stewart. These names alone, selected as friends and intimates, mark Creech as a man of no common attainments.

At this period the beautiful Duchess of Gordon was at the head of social fashion and the elite were honoured in being her invited guests. Lord Monboddo was another social leader, and held a place alone for his dinners. Allan Cunningham, referring to these banquets, tells us that Lord Monboddo " desired to revive the splendid suppers of the ancients, and place on his tables the choicest of wines, in decanters of a Grecian pattern, adorned with wreaths of flowers : painting lent its attraction as well as music, while odours of all kinds were diffused from visible or invisible sources."

The Earl of Glencairn, a warm friend and generous patron of the poet, and a man of considerable influence in the Scotland of the eighteenth century, was in great measure responsible for Creech issuing the Edinburgh Burns. Even so, the cultured, shining Henry Mackenzie, the leading personality of all the brilliant fellowship, made the task easy by his article in the *Lounger* which at once gave the poet his status amongst the elite. When the Creech edition was finally issued from the press, the name of Robert Burns was for all time assured. To William Creech the Burns lover owes a deep debt of gratitude, and one might almost be permitted to take a liberty with Sir Walter Scott and, substituting the name Creech for that which he mentions (Henry Mackenzie), take as a concluding note the passage : " the last link in the chain which connected the Scottish Literature of the present age with the period when there were giants in the land—the days of Robertson, Hume, Smith, Home, Clark, and Ferguson."

While we have progressed and forged ahead in almost every direction, while life of to-day must be judged as on an altogether higher and better plane, to look calmly back on the figures that thronged the old High Street of Edinburgh, or to study in our quiet hours the rich literary legacy they have left us, is to realise that life has in truth passed on, but it has also left the witty, lettered golden age far behind.   Perhaps it is slight exaggeration to borrow a Henry Williamson phrase and refer to " this transitional age of thwarted hope and mental fear," but there was a certain dignity, a marked personality amongst the leading men of that other age.   Individual thought, not the mass mind, was of some value and importance, and then as now, minorities were generally in the right.

With the passing of William Creech on January 14, 1815, in the seventieth year of a full and complete life, the old Greyfriars kirkyard received another of that older generation who did so much to found the character and reputation on which the Scotland of to-day is known to the outside world.

# SIR ALEXANDER BOSWELL, Bart.,

## of Auchinleck

WHENEVER the name Boswell is mentioned the mind instinctively flies to the biographer of Dr. Johnson. That is one of the penalties attached to all bearers of a great name ; they are oftentimes judged and appraised by an altogether wrong standard. It has been said of James Boswell, by more than one student of his times, that far from being a genius, he was not even a particularly able man ; but the fact remains that his life of Johnson is still to-day the standard by which such work is judged. And it would be strange if such an ancient house as that of Auchinleck did not produce more than one son of outstanding ability, if for no other reason than for that love of books which appears to have been bred in their bones. From the early days of the seventeenth century—and we need not go further back—until the branch of the family we are now dealing with became extinct about a hundred years ago, literature, as a study and creative art, was almost an integral part of their lives.

As a family name, the Boswells trace their history back to the days of William the Conqueror. The Auchinleck branch has not such a long association with Kyle, but even so, their roots are planted deep. We read that the lands were granted to Thomas Boswell by James IV, but he could not long have enjoyed the lairdship, because, in common with so many, he lost his life on Flodden field.

But the history of Scottish families of rank is a confusing matter unless one has space to enlarge upon the subject in an unnecessary and lengthy manner. Suffice it to say that Boswells occupied the land of Auchinleck long before the days of the Thomas Boswell referred to. A laird of that name and designation took his place by the side of William Wallace in the Scottish wars for freedom.

The family tree and its ramifications need not detain us ; the only reason for referring to it at all is to show that in Sir Alexander we are not treating with a self-made man who had to struggle for recognition. Here was a man born into high estate ; gifted above most, with all the educational advantages the age could afford, and with the added fact that as the eldest son of the Biographer his audience was waiting. Lord Auchinleck, a Senator of the College of Justice, was his grandfather ; a man noted for his ability as a lawyer and scholar, but a strict Presbyterian and Whig of a type now extinct.

The old Lord was vastly upset when he discovered that his slightly erratic son, James, had attached himself to Dr. Johnson. It is easy to-day for us to understand why. We can see the wide, unbridgeable gulf which was bound to exist between the views of two such strong, self-opinionated men. On the one hand, the proud old aristocrat, occupying a position of very real importance in Scotland, more often consulted than contradicted, and deferred to even by his equals ; and that at a time when Edinburgh was practically alone in representing the culture and society of our country. Then take Johnson, with his boorish manners and rugged exterior ; his opinion of the Scots, their religious observances, and his loud intolerance of anyone who dared to hold divergent views.

As one would expect, the two men did not *draw*. The uncompromising old Lord of Session was much incensed at the friendship, and on one occasion, when conversing with a friend who made enquiries about his son's welfare, Lord Auchinleck is said to have replied : " There's nae hope for Jamie, man ! Jamie has gane clean gyte . . . . whose tail do you think he has pinned himself to now, man ? A *dominie*, man, an auld dominie ; he keepit a *school* and called it an *academy* "—a diatribe worthy of the Doctor himself !

With such a grandfather, and the son of a celebrated father, Alexander Boswell could hardly fail to be a man of marked personality.    His mother, a woman of sound judgment and no little character, was a daughter of Sir Walter Montgomerie of Lainshaw, another well-known Ayrshire family.

Alexander was the elder of two brothers, and was born on October 9, 1775.    He was educated in England, first at Westminster School, and then at Oxford University. In 1795, his father, James Boswell, died, and Alexander, then a youth in his twentieth year, fell heir to the estate. As was the custom, in his station of life, young Boswell made the grand tour of Europe, and then on his return settled down at Auchinleck to live the life of a Scottish county gentleman.    To a man of his tastes, Auchinleck was the ideal environment.    He was now owner of one of the most valuable private libraries in existence, and in every sense quite independent of the outside world, free to pursue his studies at his leisure.

Once, through the influence of a friend, I was given the freedom of Auchinleck to wander and explore at will. The entrance gate looks bleak and uninteresting, but once inside the cold exterior is forgotten.    No matter how divergent the outlook or taste, almost everyone would find something of interest in Auchinleck grounds.    Ancient trees, some quite unusual and bound in wire to enable them

SIR ALEXANDER BOSWELL.

to bear their weight of years ; gardens, and an old-time bowling green, not to omit the famous library which, alas ! I did not see.

One remarkable feature lies in the fact that the progress of the Auchinleck family can here be traced in discarded residences. First there are the remains of the original stronghold, built on an upstanding rock, the Lugar flowing far below its natural walls, a place almost impregnable in its time. Next the old house, sign of a growing civilisation, still stout enough to give security but with an added degree of comfort. And then the present house of Auchinleck, built in the Grecian style, and erected in 1780 by Lord Auchinleck, father of James Boswell of the Johnson associations.

To all this, then, Alexander Boswell fell heir, to use and enjoy as he considered best. He turned his mind to letters ; and not merely did he write, and write some very good stuff, too, but also he installed a printing press and issued some of his own original work and, equally valuable, reissued some of the old and otherwise unavailable volumes from his library. One contribution to our out-of-the-way literature of another age which but for Boswell would have remained immured in Auchinleck library, was the issue in 1812 of a facsimile copy of the black-letter original of the debate between John Knox and Abbot Quentin Kennedy. This disputation was staged in Maybole in 1562, and the volume in question was given to the world by one of the protagonists, the great John Knox. After some correspondence as to where they should meet to argue about their theological dogmas, the capital of Carrick was mutually agreed upon. Each principal was supported by forty adherents. As a personal observation, I may say they must have formed a thoroughly uncomfortable congregation in the room at their disposal, which is still there to be examined. The proceedings lasted for three days and were then brought to an inconclusive termination. The truth of the matter is that Maybole was unable to bear the strain of feeding such a number of guests, so the debate was adjourned for lack of provisions ! Kennedy was the last of the Crossraguel abbots, and was succeeded in the Church lands by that Allan Stewart who figured as the centrepiece of the savage Black Vault of Dunure drama. But we deviate from our main subject.

From the treasures of the famous library, too, Sir Walter Scott collected the romance *Sir Tristram*, judged by him as the earliest example of Scottish poetry in existence.

But Boswell's literary name was not founded by burrowing amongst the works of other minds. On my shelves are three slim volumes of which he is author. One of these is entitled *Songs, Chiefly in the Scottish Dialect*, and was published by Manners & Miller, Edinburgh, 1803. The preface is short and to the point : " Several of the following songs have been printed in Edinburgh and Glasgow without the Author's permission, and with alterations which he did not consider as improvements, he has been induced to present them to the Public in a more correct form." Amongst the contents are one or two songs which had their vogue, and even now the titles at least are familiar to most Scots, notably " Jenny's Bawbee " and " Jenny Dang the Weaver." There is also included an item entitled " Song, to an Irish Air, by the late James Boswell, Esq.," the opening line of which reads, " O Larghan Clanbrassil, how sweet is thy sound." The most interesting section is some supplementary pages bound in at the end and entitled " Scraps, written by the late Sir A. B., from a MS. in his Handwriting." The final item in his section consists of some rather cynical verses on " Old Q."

My two other volumes, attenuated and odd in shape, were issued by the Auchinleck Press in 1816. The larger is *Skildon Haughs*. This is a rhymed account of the flitting of the Sow, an Ayrshire feudal escapade between he Craufords and the Kennedies. The tale—an amusing incident as viewed at this distance—is well known to those interested in west country tradition, thanks to Sir Alexander, who got the story from George Rankine of Whitehill, and by his pen made it live for us who were to follow.

When in 1817, Joseph Train dined with Sir Walter Scott in Castle Street, Boswell was included amongst the guests, and on that occasion he proudly handed a copy of his book to the great novelist with the remark that it had been written, printed and bound by himself.

The third volume in my possession deals with an altogether different type of adventure and is entitled *The Woo-Creel; or The Bull o' Bashan*.

The collected poetical works of Sir Alexander were issued in one modern volume in 1871, but the verses commented upon as the third volume have, perhaps wisely, been omitted from the book.

Although interested in literary matters, a gifted and highly educated man, Sir Alexander was no bookworm. He was, indeed, keenly a votary of all field sports, a good shot, ardent fisherman, and at one time evidently a devotee of the turf. Later he gave up racing and devoted some time to hunting, and for several seasons he maintained his own pack of hounds. In his day coursing was another popular sport, and in this, too, he joined with zest. That he was a curler, considering his environment, goes without saying, even had we not actual proof, because no one but an experienced votary of the roaring game could have composed " Lochside and Damback." Every move in the game, every phrase associated with the bonspiel, are introduced, and the chorus alone proves the devotee :

> When snaw lies white on ilka knowe,
> The ice-stane and the good broom kowe
> Can warm us like a bleezin' lowe—
> Fair fa' the ice and curlin'.

Collectors know the value of the Auchinleck and Cumnock snuff-mulls. These originated through the visit of a Frenchman to Auchinleck. Something went wrong with this alien's snuff-mull, and a local craftsman, being asked to try his skill at repairing it, discovered the secret of the hinge, and thus a one-time thriving and important industry was started.

Naturally, as an Ayrshire laird of literary bent, Boswell was a keen admirer of Burns. Perhaps worshippers of that poet are under a greater debt to Auchinleck than they generally admit. In any case the cenotaph on the banks of the Doon owes its inception to his enthusiasm. Realising the desire for some such memorial, Sir Alexander convened a meeting, in Ayr, of all parties likely to be interested in the project. Only one person attended. Nothing daunted, Sir Alexander took the chair, appointed his solitary audience of one as honorary secretary, and proceeded to give his address and draft resolutions. He then drew up a minute of the proceedings and sent it to all the leading newspapers. This publicity attracted attention ; others came to his aid, and soon a full and energetic committee was formed and a sum of over £3,000 raised. On the poet's birthday, January 25, 1820, Sir Alexander had the pleasure of laying the foundation-stone, and his address on that occasion is even yet a model of well-chosen words.

About this time, covering a period of some years, the whole industrial section of the community was passing through a season of unrest, in many parts amounting to armed insurrection. The deeds they committed led to the Reform Bill of 1832, but previous to that Act the country was seething with discontent and the outlook was serious.

For the part he played in upholding law and order, Mr. Alexander Boswell, as he then was, had the dignity of a Baronetcy conferred upon him in 1821, and no man was ever more worthy of a title. Unfortunately, he was not long to enjoy his new status. Political feelings ran high, and those who entered the lists were not, at that time, quite so observant of good taste, or perhaps had not so much to fear from the law of libel. Sir Alexander entered into the political storm with all his wonted fire and enthusiasm. He was a Tory, and every talent at his disposal was freely given to his side. A squib entitled " A New Whig Song " appeared in the *Glasgow Sentinel*. It rhymed with the name Stuart and was pointed and deliberately offensive. Jumping to conclusions, James Stuart of Dunearn imputed Boswell of being the author. Unfortunately for all concerned in the affair, Sir Alexander had been called to London where his only brother was lying dangerously ill. He travelled by stage-coach, a slow and tedious journey, and instead of having even a few last words with one he loved so well he actually got there only in time to attend the funeral. On his return, another long and weary experience, plunged in gloom and sorrow, he was given a letter from the Earl of Rosslyn asking for an appointment. This was granted without delay, when the Earl explained that he was acting for Mr. Stuart, and he must request Sir Alexander either to deny any connection with the verses or to meet his principal in a duel. Boswell, bowed with sorrow and weary with travel, listened in silence and did not even reply

The affair of honour had now to go on, and after the usual arrangements had been completed, Stuart and Boswell met in a field in Auchtertrool, Fife. Sir Alexander made his position quite clear to his friends, and stated that he would fire in the air. In this he was as good as his word, but unfortunately his opponent did not take such a generous view ; Boswell fell mortally wounded, and died the following afternoon, March 26th, 1822. Stuart was arrested, but after trial was honourably acquitted.

Thus died Sir Alexander Boswell in his forty-seventh year. What he might have achieved had he lived the normal span is mere speculation, but that he had unusual intellect and ability is without doubt. Ayrshire lost an outstanding son, Scotland a potentially great figure, by his untimely passing.

DUNCAN FORBES of Culloden.

# DUNCAN FORBES OF CULLODEN

## Judge and Patriot

OF all the outstanding episodes in Scottish history, none is more interesting, perhaps because of its colour and romance, than the ill-fated Stuart rising of 1745. Prince Charles Edward Stuart is either a hero or a rebel according to the reader's viewpoint. His romantic arrival on the west coast, the rallying of the clans to his support, the tricking of Cope and the descent to the lowlands : the light-hearted days in Holyrood, followed by the swift, sudden victory at Prestonpans, have been used as the pattern for a tartan garment of romance. Skirling warpipes, flashing claymores, the white cockade, lend a glamour to the movement and make it an inexhaustible store for poet and novelist.

Of course, we to-day see events of two hundred years ago from the security of our firesides. Time has mellowed the harshness, concealed the cruelties, gilded the ferocity and selfishness. It was not romance in 1745. There was no more romance at Culloden than there was at Mons, apart from the fact that two hundred years have tuned it and added grace notes far removed from the original.

In this connection two men stood out in bold relief amongst their fellows : the Prince and the Duke of Cumberland. They were leaders in the field—and the Duke won. Both had their adherents, but neither was an altogether flawless character. Bonnie Prince Charlie was weak and vacillating ; indeed a man better fitted for the task might have carried the day, but the fact remains that in his dark hour he evinced a strain of courage almost heroic.

Victory did little to alter his rival, Cumberland; it merely offered him an opportunity to make a more public display of the callous, brutal temperament that stamped him. The man who would pilfer the linen and silver from his lodgings in Aberdeen, on his way north, was not likely to have much natural feeling for an enemy given into his power on the battlefield.

As always, behind the principal figures stand a host of other men of varying mentalities, ranging from splendid clear-sighted leaders to blustering fools, as has been the unvarying rule in all movements since the world took form. Many of these men are familiar to all : their names are recorded in history : their deeds are enshrined—or derided —in song. Amidst the welter of kilts and red coats the more sombre garb of Duncan Forbes is apt to be overlooked ; yet had his counsel been listened to, his advice been given weight, whatever the result, the course of the '45 would have been altered.

It is so easy to look back on past deeds and to criticise; but whatever views one may hold of the '45, it will be generally agreed that a more supine government, more blundering, blustering army leaders, never at any time held power in our land. Think of poor floundering Johnny Cope and the ridiculous statesmen who were in great measure responsible for his predicaments. We have no parallel for it, with the possible exception of the last Boer war, where one might profitably draw an analogy. It is the nearest comparison I can conjure—and, come to think of it, there were many points of similarity. Here and there we come across a man of clear vision, a born counsellor but a voice crying in the wilderness. Such a man was Duncan Forbes, and had the wiseacres in office in his time paid a little more heed to his warnings, given a little more weight to his opinions, many a heart-thrilling chapter, many a haunting ballad, would be missing from our literature.

Duncan Forbes was born at Bunchrew on November 10, 1685. The county of his birth was Inverness. His father was Duncan Forbes of Culloden, so that the future Lord Advocate, and later Lord President, of the Court of Session was essentially Highland in birth and outlook. It is necessary, when appraising his words and deeds, to bear that fact in mind. Although Highland and living in the heart of the clan country, a part of Scotland which could not by any known test be considered peaceful, the Culloden family held their views on church and state manfully and openly, and in consequence were not looked upon with favour by their warlike neighbours. In a word, they were not popular with the Jacobite clans and families.

In 1689 their estates were ravaged and despoiled by Buchan and Connor, to such an extent that the loss amounted to fully fifty-four thousand pounds *Scots*. And that was not the grand total of their distress, because the Government troops sent to quell the unruly clansmen were also quartered on the lands in question, causing additional expense to Forbes, so that the cure was as ill to thole as the disease. Such was the burden pressing on him by friend and foe, that Forbes entered a claim upon the Government for £47,400, and so substantiated his claims that the Government had to admit their justice. Parliament advised the King (William III) to accede. Instead of paying compensation, the needy government of the day granted to the Forbes family the perquisite of perpetual right to distil, free of duty, from grain raised on their Ferintosh estate. As might be expected, the grant brought in a very handsome revenue, so much so that when, in 1784, the Government purchased back the rights by compulsory agreement, for

M

the sum of £21,500, the amount was considered to be quite inadequate compensation.

Young Duncan Forbes, then, was born into a scene of doubts and troubles, but his financial outlook was not one that called for too much sympathy. He was the second son and when his father died in 1704, John, his elder brother succeeded to the estates.

Of Duncan's boyhood, we have little record. One of his uncles was a lieutenant-colonel, and considering the times and the lad's position in life, it is not surprising that he was intended for an army career. Another uncle, Sir David Forbes of Newhall, was a distinguished lawyer and when Mr. Forbes died in 1704, Duncan was sent to Edinburgh to study law. After reading in the capital for a year or so he transferred to Leyden, a favourite centre with Scottish students. A young man of splendid endowments, he proved a diligent student not merely of his chosen law subjects, but also of Oriental languages. He returned to his native country in 1707, and continued his studies in Edinburgh for other two years. In July, at the age of twenty-four, he was admitted as an advocate.

There existed a strong bond of friendship between the Culloden family and the house of Argyll, and this was now to prove valuable to the young advocate. The Duke by his influence, had Duncan Forbes appointed as Sheriff of Mid-Lothian, and in addition he, and Lord Ilay, handed over to him the management of their Scottish estates, a task for which he was admirably fitted. A young man of his brilliant attainments, with such influential friends to back him, found that his success in his chosen career was immediate, and he soon built up a large practice.

With his position stabilised and his future assured he married Miss Mary Rose, a daughter of the ancient

ouse of Kilravock, and settled down to lead the busy
life of a prosperous advocate.

While on the surface all appeared to be going well,
never at any time were stronger opposing currents of policy
and intrigue at work in Scotland. The Union of 1707 was
not really a popular measure in the Lowlands, while the
Highland clans, with one or two notable exceptions, were
scheming and hoping for a Stuart restoration. The
attitude of Argyll and his Campbells was definitely known ;
while the strong bonds of friendship which existed between
the Culloden family and some of their neighbours assured
the Grants, Munroes and Rosses for the government side ;
but every other tartan—not perhaps without reason—was
suspect. This position made life precarious for the
loyalists, and the Culloden household was continually on
the watch, surrounded as they were by a ring of armed clans,
where the word of a chief was the only known law.

These were testing days for all, from castle to cot-
house, as even in the lowlands feudalism was not quite dead ;
indeed, so late as 1747, when heritable jurisdiction was
being finally abolished, the claims for compensation for
loss of rights, intimated to the Court of Session, amounted
to almost £600,000.

Munro of Fowlis, John Forbes of Culloden, and
Duncan in Edinburgh were quite alive to what was brewing.
Notwithstanding warnings and advice, the government
would not pay heed, and through official negligence and
futility were caught napping by the rising of 1715. John
Forbes, out of his private resources, paid out large sums on
behalf of the government, on public service, but when the
affair was over and the rising dispersed, the government
fell asleep again, and he was never reimbursed for his
outlay.

By now Duncan Forbes, owing to his brilliance in court work and his public life generally, was recognised as one of the leading personalities in Scotland. Notwithstanding his unpopularity with the government of the day because of his utterances against the removal of political prisoners and making them stand trial in English Courts, Forbes was too influential a man to be overlooked. In 1722 he became Member of Parliament for Inverness Burghs, and in 1725, by his undoubted abilities, was given the important office of Lord Advocate for Scotland. And now the Lord Advocate became exceedingly unpopular in Glasgow and the West. The Malt Tax was not well received in Scotland, and nowhere did it create greater dislike than on Clydeside. The people were unused to fiscal taxation and looked upon the novelty as an unwelcome fruit of the Union.

The Glasgow member was Mr. Campbell of Shawfield, a man who had taken a leading part in having the new tax imposed. It came into force on June 23, 1725, and at once there were signs of unrest, people gathering in the streets and discussing the matter. The magistrates deemed it wise to ask for a military party. This was at once supplied, in command of a Captain Bushell. Next day the mob acted and completely destroyed Shawfield House. The following morning groups started to assemble near Mr. Campbell's town house, and the military, being called out, formed a square round the M.P.'s home. A few stones were thrown, and losing his temper, Bushell ordered his troops to fire. Eight persons were killed and a considerable number wounded. The enraged citizens ran to the guard-house and took possession of the arms stored therein, while a party started to ring the town bell. So serious was the position of the troops that the provost urged them to leave the city at once, and had not Bushell led his men off to Dumbarton it is certain they would all have been slain.

And then Lord Advocate Forbes acted foolishly. Calling out a large body of soldiers in command of General Wade, he marched to Glasgow, arrested the magistrates, and, conveying them to Edinburgh, had them incarcerated in the Tolbooth. The feeling against the tax, the rancour against the government, was such that while the prisoners were being escorted along the High Street of Edinburgh, a number of prominent men walked bare-headed in the procession to prove their sympathy with the Bailies. The arrest was quickly proved to be illegal, and the Glasgow prisoners now martyrs in the eyes of their fellow-country-men, were liberated.

That was in June. In August the brewers in Edinburgh gave notice that they were ceasing to brew beer because of the tax. Several of these gentlemen soon found them-selves inside the doors of the Tolbooth, and again the capital and county generally were seething with discontent. These were troublous times for Forbes, but even more trying experiences were to follow. In 1734, on the death of his brother John, Duncan Forbes became proprietor of the family estates. No sooner had his private affairs been settled, than, in 1736, the notorious Porteous Mob surged into being, as a result of which the city was to be officially deprived of all its privileges. Forbes exerted himself to avert this public disaster, and with much exertion succeeded in securing great modifications of the punishment.

In 1737 further honour was conveyed to Forbes, the position of Lord Advocate being exchanged for that of President of the Court of Session. At once he set himself to clear up the anomalies which were in evidence. Until that time the senior judge had it in his arbitrary power to postpone a case without showing cause, so that it might come up for trial before a special judge or alternatively when someone would be absent from his place in court. Now the new Lord President ruled that all cases must be taken up as they came upon the Roll, a distinct move towards fair trial for every one concerned.   But now blacker clouds, unobserved by most, were creeping over the national horizon.   The affair of '15 may have been forgotten by the government, but the embers still smouldered amongst the Jacobite factions.

In 1742 the Stuart supporters sent a missive to Rome, pledging themselves to do all in their power to restore the Stuarts to the throne.

Forbes was too busy with Court of Session matters to keep in close touch with political intrigue, until a letter from a friend in the Highlands advised him that Prince Charles had actually landed and that the clans were rallying to his support.   Without delay the Lord President warned the authorities of the gravity of the situation, and then hurried north to his native Culloden to exert his influence towards thwarting the proposed rebellion.   His personal friendship with many of the Highland chiefs likely to be implicated, his influence as a great landowner, and his official position in the state, all combined to make his presence in Inverness unwelcome and embarrassing.

Some of those who in their hearts were anxious for the success of the Stuart cause felt impelled, by strong ties, not to break openly with their powerful friend.   Lord Lovat was amongst the first to call and consult with him about the position.   Macdonald of Skye and Macleod of Macleod wrote assuring him of their loyalty.   There is no doubt that the influence of Duncan Forbes did much to hold in check the rising flood which otherwise might have swept all before it. And then, poor Johnny Cope, tricked and out-manœuvred, opened the way for the clan's march towards the south.

This apparent success had its immediate effect in the north and made the position at Culloden, to say the least, precarious. The Frasers put into operation a plan for taking Forbes prisoner and so wrecking the only government link which existed across the Highland line. Of course, the Lord President was too much alive to his danger, too closely in touch with affairs, to be surprised, and the attack upon his house was beaten off. When Lovat found that one or two strong clans had not merely refused to join the Jacobites, but were actually marching towards the protection of their friends at Culloden, the wily old fox repudiated all connection with the attack but made restitution of the cattle driven off and laid the blame at the door of his impetuous lieutenants.

Forbes contributed money from his own private fortune, borrowing where he could, and contrived to do much—more perhaps than will ever be known—to hold in check the restless spirits whose hearts were with the Stuart cause, and at least restrain them from taking active part against the Hanoverian side. His ill-requited exertions, the drain upon his resources, physical and financial, the obligations he had entered into with his friends, and the cold-blooded neglect on the part of London, broke down health and spirit and ultimately ended in his death, a man worn out in doing what he considered to be his duty. On December 10, 1747, Lord President Duncan Forbes died in his sixty-second year. His last days must have been embittered by the cruel enactments of the government forces after Drumossie. Although himself loyal to the side he considered in the right, he had friends by ties of blood and old associations among many of those who suffered so cruelly. By every instinct he was a Highlander, and the sorry treatment of those, even as a result of their own deeds, whom he had so often counselled and advised and had met in social hours, and whose friendship he respected, was enough to sour a harder nature than he possessed.

Two years after Duncan Forbes' death the tardy government bestowed a pension of £400 a year for life upon his son. A poor enough reward for all that the family had done and sacrificed. Whatever may be the reader's private opinion of the ill-fated '45 and all connected with it, everyone who has taken thought to study the events which led up to it, the conduct of the campaign from the Stuart or from the Hanoverian angle, will admit that throughout the whole dark chapter Duncan Forbes of Culloden played the part of an honest, upright man.

ROBERT FERGUSSON.

# ROBERT FERGUSSON

## A Scottish Poet

Ramsay and famous Fergusson
Gied Forth and Tay a lift aboon

THESE lines are a quotation from Burns—and the "famous Fergusson" is a tribute to a man who, amongst the general reading public at least, has never been accorded his proper place or value. To many he is a name and nothing more.

The life of Robert Fergusson was a tragedy. Indeed, in the whole history of Scottish letters there is no more distressing chapter. Gifted to the point of genius, he died in a public asylum, alone, on a bed of straw, on the eve of completing his twenty-fourth year. What an environment for any man, even the most callous—but this was a highly-strung youth of fine sensibilities, and the greatest poet of his day. No wonder the man best equipped by nature to understand his mental anguish, and in whom there was such an affinity of outlook, Robert Burns, when he visited Edinburgh, knelt on Fergusson's grave and could not restrain his tears.

R. L. Stevenson writes somewhere that Fergusson lived again in him—and I think he believed it.

The reader will admit that there must be some outstanding merit in the man Fergusson to move so deeply the imagination of two such immortal figures. And these two were not alone in their appraisement. Andrew Lang once made the public utterance : "There is Fergusson, Burns's master, who died at twenty-four, but so unfortunate after death, as in life, that I doubt if we have a proper critical edition." Of course, that is over-praise. Fergusson, with all his ability, was not the " master " of Robert Burns ; he was not the equal of the Ayrshire poet, but what he might have achieved had he lived is a conjecture that leaves us wondering—unfruitful speculation, perhaps, leading nowhere, but sometimes a haunting thought !

There was much in common between the two poets, Fergusson and Burns. Each had for mother a woman of strong religious character. The father of each was a staunch, upright man, perhaps too fine metal to stand the hard strain of life ; certainly too just and upright in walk to bow to anything questionable. We know how want and poverty embittered and spoiled the life of the old Ayrshire farmer. The records at our disposal tell us that William Fergusson never earned above twenty-five pounds a year. We can only wonder and sympathise ; it is difficult for the average man to understand. When we trace all the facts at our disposal, and attempt to follow either of the two poets in his wayward path, if we have any human qualities in our hearts we can only look on and echo the words of Burns :

> O ye douce folk, that live by rule,
> Grave, tideless-blooded, calm and cool,
> Compared wi' you—O fool ! fool ! fool !
> How much unlike
> Your hearts are just a standing pool,
> Your lives a dyke.

Not that I am apologising for Robert Fergusson, or for Robert Burns either for that part of it, because a greater man than either wrote : " The evil that men do lives after them " ; but he might have added that cleanminded men do not love to grope amongst the garbage.

Robert Fergusson was born in Edinburgh on September 5, 1750. The house of his birth was demolished when the modern North Bridge came into being, but in any case the Cap-and-Feather close—the title by which its site was known—was not a very salubrious neighbourhood. While he came of good Aberdeenshire stock—for some generations his family had resided in the Tarland district—Robert Fergusson was a delicate child. For that reason he was much later in being sent to school than was usual in Scottish homes. His mother, afraid of his health, preferred to teach him his letters at the fireside, and proved very successful at the task. When at last he was enrolled as a pupil at a private school, it meant little to the Edinburgh laddie that almost immediately opposite his class-room was the shop of Allan Ramsay, a name which he, in common with most of his contemporaries in later life, was to hold in reverence as that of a master.

Fergusson's parents were fully alive to the desirability, indeed the necessity, for giving their delicate boy a sound education, and so in due course Robert was taken away from the little private academy and entered at the High School. There was then no better school in the country, but the rules were of a spartan nature such as would to-day be considered a hardship by even the most robust. Classes opened at seven in the morning, and with an hour for breakfast went on uninterruptedly until noon. After the dinner interval there followed a further three hours of schooling,—in all a long, heavy day.

The boy proved a quick and ready scholar, and although he suffered much from broken time owing to bad health, was a studious, intelligent lad and did well in his classes.

When his term at the High School had been completed, Robert Fergusson, at the behest of his parents, sat an examination for a bursary, the winning of which would enable him to carry on his studies and so qualify for entering a profession. That profession, his mother fondly hoped, would be the Church. When the result of the examination was announced, Fergusson was one of the two successful entrants. By the terms of the bequest, this necessitated the boy entering the Grammar School of Dundee, and going later, if his record proved diligence and application, for a period at the University of St. Andrews.

In those days even the short journey from Edinburgh to Dundee was an adventure, and for a delicate boy of eleven something of an ordeal. After three years in Dundee, his record there having been all that was required, in his fourteenth year Fergusson was enrolled as a student in the University town. His boyhood years behind him—in a scholastic sense that is, for he was still but a lad—he was now a University student. The " auld grey toon " of St. Andrews has changed very much since Fergusson's time. Still, it was a seat of learning, and the young poet had now every chance to fit himself for his appointed profession. It is interesting to find how the youthful divinity student appeared to his fellows, what type of person he really was. Here is a quotation from Hugh Miller :

"Among the students of the upper classes, however, there was at least one individual with whom I longed to be acquainted. He was apparently much about my own age, rather below than above the middle size, and rather delicately than robustly formed ; but I have rarely seen a more elegant figure or more interesting face. His features were small, and there was what might perhaps be described as a too feminine delicacy in the whole contour ; but there was a broad and very high expanse of forehead, which, even in those days, when we were acquainted with only the phrenology taught by Plato, might be regarded as the index of a capacious and powerful mind ; and the brilliant light of his large dark eyes seemed to give earnest of its activity.

" Who, in the name of wonder, is that ? " I inquired of a class-fellow, as this interesting-looking young man passed me for the first time.

" A clever but very unsettled fellow from Edinburgh," replied the lad, " a capital linguist, for he gained our first bursary three years ago ; but our professor says he is certain he will never do any good. He cares nothing for the company of scholars like himself ; and employs himself—though he excels, I believe, in English composition—in writing vulgar Scotch rhymes like Allan Ramsay. His name is Robert Fergusson."

But he was a very human lad for all that, and some of his ploys and pranks have been handed down to us. In the days before church organs were introduced, musical praise was led by the precentor. I fancy that most people of mature years will have personal recollections of some church where instrumental music was either taboo or where the congregation was not financially in a position to instal an " American organ." I have still vivid recollections of the precentor in the church I attended when a boy. When the psalm was announced from the pulpit, the precentor rose, and taking a tuning-fork from his waistcoat pocket and finding the correct pitch, he advanced to the rails, faced the congregation, and commenced to bawl forth the first verse in a raucous voice while the assembled worshippers waveringly joined and ultimately drowned the leader as they gathered confidence. Fergusson was gifted with a sweet singing voice, and so was appointed precentor to lead the praise on Sunday when the students in the College chapel were at worship. The position was a distasteful one to him, as it would be to most normal youths ; but discipline was adamant, and week after week he was forced to undergo the mental torture. On the day in question it was further customary, when any one was ill or unable for a particular reason to attend divine service, to send a message to the minister asking for the prayers and intercession of the congregation on his or her behoof. This " line," as it was termed, was read out by the precentor before the principal prayer.

This was to be Fergusson's avenue of escape. One Sabbath morning, taking his place at the reading desk, with a solemn countenance he requested those assembled to " remember in prayer, a young man, now present, of whom, from the sudden effects of inebriety, there appears but small hope of recovery." Picture the amazement of the grave professors, the titters of the students, at such an indecorous act ! But it had the desired effect, and from that day Fergusson was relieved of the office he so much detested.

His reckless courage was again illustrated and in an even more amazing way. Fergusson, as we have mentioned, was a bursar-student, and was forced to take his turn with those of that category in " saying a blessing " before meals. The food was not particularly good, and moreover suffered from that lack of variety which is so necessary for full enjoyment of the table. The youthful poet brooded over the fact, and one dinner-hour, when it was his turn to invoke a grace, he rose and, with a solemn visage, recited :

> For rabbits young and for rabbits old,
> For rabbits hot and for rabbits cold,
> For rabbits tender and for rabbits tough,
> Our thanks we render, for we've had enough.

Once again the authorities were shocked at such temerity, but the " graceless blessing," if one may coin a phrase, was effective in results. Rabbit ceased to figure as an almost daily dish, and so justified was the satire, that on this occasion Fergusson was not even admonished.

Much has been said and written about the drinking customs of the eighteenth century, but like another, and be it said a greater poet, Robert Fergusson was no drunkard. The passing of time means in many instances that a man is judged by his legacy—his literary fancies—rather than by his actual deeds when in the flesh. It is understandable, but rather unfortunate, that this should be so, but we must accept the facts of life as they are.

No one who lived in St. Andrews a century and a half ago would, if he could return, recognise the clean old-world town of to-day as compared with its then appearance and atmosphere. When Heron visited it on his Tour there were more than one hundred and fifty ale and dram shops, and the houses were not very creditable to the native population. Chevalier Johnstone passed the stricture that " no town ever so much deserved the fate of *Sodom and Gomorrah* "—and that is not the most vitriolic sentence ! Judged by modern standards of sanitation, mental and physical, of moral outlook and social customs, the town of St. Andrews was no worse than its neighbours ; but the point is that a young lad, intellectual and temperamental, must not be placed in the dock of public opinion and judged by standards entirely foreign to his day and generation. Much that is exaggerated has been written about his drinking habits, but, judged by the social customs of the time, the criticisms are unfair and unwarranted.

In 1767, before his term of University life was run, Robert Fergusson's father died, of asthma. His modest earnings, and his sacrifices to give each one of his family the benefit of a good education, resulted in the position that William Fergusson did not leave his widow any too well provided with this world's gear. Robert's elder brother had already left home in his adopted calling as a seaman, and now it was necessary for the student to lay aside his projected career in the Church and to find some work which would help to support his mother.

The family hopes were now vested in John Forbes, Mrs. Fergusson's brother, and a man of considerable wealth and position, laird of several farms in Aberdeenshire. In 1769, a month or two after finally saying good-bye to St. Andrews and his University career, Robert Fergusson visited his uncle, the visit, be it made clear, being by invitation from that gentleman himself. His reception seems to have been generous enough; but instead of using his influence or exerting himself in any way to find employment for his brilliant, well-educated and orphaned nephew, Forbes went about his own affairs and did not trouble. Robert Fergusson was a poor lad, from a tragically poor home, and after living with his uncle for some months, his clothes became somewhat threadbare. Forbes, rather ungraciously, intimated that fact to the lad, and pointed out that he was not dressed in keeping with the house in which he was residing. To a high-spirited boy this was too much. Robert at once left his uncle's house; repairing to a neighbouring inn, he penned a letter in strong, manly sentiments, and arranging for its delivery to his uncle, he started off, with empty pockets, to tramp the long miles to his mother's house in Edinburgh.

On receipt of the letter, Forbes, struck with a shallow remorse at his own mean action, despatched a messenger after his nephew with a few shillings to help him on his

ourney.   When at length Fergusson reached Edinburgh,
underfed, footsore and weary, ashamed of the cause of
his return, and worrying about his mother, he took to his
bed, a wreck for the time-being.

Employment of some kind was now an urgent need,
and when he recovered from his unfortunate experience,
Fergusson set about securing a position to stave off the
pressing family necessities.    Some good Edinburgh
friends used their influence on his behalf, and he obtained
employment as a clerk in the Commissary-Clerk's office—
not a post to serve the ideal of one of such brilliant gifts,
but at least a wage-earning security.    True to promise and
training, he assiduously devoted his time to his employer's
interests ;  but his evenings were free, and these he must
have used to advantage or the legacy he has left to literature
and the world had never been accomplished.    The few
years of his life were passing, but January, 1772, saw his
position as a poet firmly established when his poem *The
Daft Days* was published.    In a month or two there followed
the *Elegy on the Death of Scots Music*, and his name was
enrolled for all time amongst the great in Scottish letters.

The poems appeared originally in the *Weekly Magazine
or Edinburgh Amusements*, published by the brothers
Ruddiman.    Each number was issued at three halfpence,
and all the prominent literary men of the time contributed.
Until 1771 there is no signed contribution from the pen of
Robert Fergusson.

The first of the poems mentioned—*The Daft Days*—
made an immediate appeal to a wide public.    The daft
days in Scotland may be compared with the Christmas
spirit in England, and the period embraced Yule, or
Christmas Day ;  Hogmanay ;  New Year's Day ;  and
Hansel Monday, the first Monday in the year.    Issued

N

while the daft days were actually being celebrated, the line
caught the public fancy, although the intrinsic value of th
poem was of itself sufficient to turn all eyes in the youn
poet's direction. The poem consisted of eleven verses—
too long to quote in full ; but here are three which go t
show the craftsman hand of the youthful clerk who wa
now to become a public figure :

> Now mirk December's dowie face
> Glowers owr the rigs wi' sour grimace,
> While thro' his MINIMUM of space
>     The blear-ey'd sun,
> Wi' blinkin' light and stealing pace,
>     His race doth run.
>
> Fiddlers, your pins in temper fix,
> And roset well your fiddlesticks,
> But banish vile Italian tricks
>     From out your quorum,
> Nor fortes wi' pianos mix—
>     Gie's Tullochgorum.
>
> Let mirth abound, let social cheer,
> Invest the dawning of the year,
> Let blithesome innocence appear
>     To crown our joy :
> Nor envy, wi' sarcastic sneer,
>     Our bliss destroy.

The *Elegy on the Death of Scots Music* also struck a
note which appealed. As the title conveys, this poem
laments the death of Scots music and merely proves how
everything in this world moves in cycles, because Fergusson,
almost two hundred years ago, voices a sentiment very
much alive to-day :

On Scotia's plains, in days of yore,
When lads and lasses tartan wore,
Soft music ran on ilka shore
      In hamely weid ;
But Harmony is now no more,
      And Music dead.

O Scotland ! that could yence afford
To bang the pith of Roman sword,
Winna your sons, wi' joint accord,
      To battle speed,
And fight till Music be restor'd
      Which now lies dead ?

Now came the years of Fergusson's poetic activity—the all-too-short years upon which his name and fame rests. Had he continued, as he started, writing in pure English, it is a matter of opinion whether his name would to-day be remembered. Fortunately he adopted the Scots dialect, with such results that as his verses appeared they were copied by other magazines and newspapers throughout the land—and a new national poet was born.

And, as Campbell writes, " He could now rank among his friends the first characters of his time in the metropolis of Scotland. His heart was open and sincere ; he was modest, but not reserved ; good natured, but not to excess ; full of vivacity and vigour of intellect, and in short, he was the most joyous and covetable companion Sociality had to boast."

One needs but to turn to Chambers's *Traditions of Edinburgh,* and to other works of like nature, to realise what was implied when Fergusson became a " Knight " in the Cape Club. From the uncongenial drudgery of the dark, candlelit office, he repaired of an evening to the laughter and social joys of Johnny Dow's or Luckie Middlemass's

taverns, the Cape Club (in which his title was " Sir Precentor," probably because of his fine singing voice), and
the theatre, where he was usually given a seat of honour in
what was known to the patrons as the Shakespeare box.
And yet his spare time cannot all have been passed in
conviviality, because now no issue of the *Magazine* appeared
without his poem.   Chambers informs us that Fergusson
reaped no pecuniary benefit from his writings, but for once
that authority is wrong.   When in 1773 the collected
verses were issued in book form, the poet had a balance to
his credit of fifty pounds.   That may not appear a large
sum, but it was a fortune to the poor clerk, trained and bred
in such straitened conditions.   In addition, he was not
merely paid in cash by Ruddiman for his contribution, but
he also received two new suits of clothes yearly.

Fergusson's love of practical jokes, the results of which
we saw in St. Andrews, never deserted him during his
sane life.   It has been remarked that he was possessed of
a fine singing voice.   One evening, as the result of a wager
about the public's love of music, he undertook to sell a
given number of printed ballads in the streets within the
stipulated time of two hours.   Disguising himself in a
long travelling coat and an old wig, he sallied forth, and
by means of his fine voice quickly collected a crowd in the
High-street.   He soon sold out his stock, and returned to
his companions, when the proceeds of the sale, and the
amount of the wager, were consumed in a merry evening.

From time to time Fergusson made excursions into the
country, chiefly to get away from the social nets which he
felt were ensnaring him, but always he was forced by
circumstances to return and fall a victim to those who
lionised him to his detriment.   One day he went to
Haddington, and while pensively walking in the church-

yard he was discovered by the Rev. John Brown. They had a chat together, and the old minister turned the conversation towards those who waste their opportunities and neglect the proper use of their talents in profitless gaiety and licence. The interview made a deep impression on Fergusson's mind, and on his return to the city he decided to lead a more austere life.

Sudden conversions are not as a rule permanent, and it was not until some time had passed that the remarks of the kindly old Haddington divine were again brought vividly to the poet's mind. Someone had given him a starling, and Fergusson, with his love of nature, became very much attached to it. One night a cat gained access to the room and seized the bird. Its cries awoke the poet, but too late to save his feathered pet. And then he remembered the parting words spoken to him at Haddington : " I will come on thee as a thief, and thou shalt not know what hour I will come upon thee."

The trifling incident, the remembered text, preyed upon his mind and changed his whole outlook. He refused to meet his friends, burned all his unpublished work, and devoted himself to reading the scriptures. Never very robust, his health suffered, and one evening he had the misfortune to stumble and fall on a staircase and knock his head. When discovered he was insensible. On being taken home, poor Fergusson, when he recovered consciousness, was found to be so affected mentally that there was no alternative to keeping him under restraint.

Two of his most intimate friends called upon him with a sedan chair and insisted that he should accompany them to make a visit. When they arrived at their destination Fergusson at once discovered where he had been taken, and a painful scene ensued. In the morning, when his mother and sister called, he had just removed a crown of straw and had been acting as if he were a king. For two months the poet was interned in circumstances which to-day would not be tolerated, but which were quite usual at that time. Hugh Miller described the place : " It was a Golgotha, which, with more than the horrors of the grave, had neither its rest nor its silence."

It would serve no good end to continue this scene. Here, alone in the night, Robert Fergusson, the poet died, on October 16, 1774, in the twenty-fourth year of his age. A mere boy—and yet, as has been said, when the great Robert Burns visited Edinburgh for the first time he made a pilgrimage to the youthful poet's grave and could not restrain his tears. A boy of twenty-four years, yet a name illustrious in the literary annals of our country. What a mystery is life !

# LORD BRAXFIELD

## Scotland's Hanging Judge

SOME of the men who held power, or achieved fame, a century and a half ago, could not possibly don ermine in our land to-day. Public opinion simply would not stand for them and their outrageous works, the manner in which they not only rode rough-shod over the conventions, but also outraged public decency.

When we ponder this fact, we realize that bad as we may consider the present-day world, we have, as a collective society, advanced in moral outlook. To no public office can these remarks more aptly be applied than to the Bench, a provision founded to give every citizen of whatever class or caste, of every age and manner of life, a fair and honest trial if brought to assize. It is only fair to state that in almost every case a prisoner in our country is looked upon as innocent until convicted by overwhelming evidence and sentence passed. We not merely expect, we know that to be so ; and we accept it as a matter of course. Public opinion is rarely outraged by a miscarriage of justice, and if a mistake sometimes creeps in, it is such an unusual circumstance that at once an outcry is raised in the newspapers and the prisoner is set free, if need be with suitable compensation. Even in such cases the fault rarely lies at the door of the judge, but in wrongous evidence or in misunderstanding of facts and clues.

So scrupulously fair are our judicial methods that a man's past record is not disclosed until his present guilt has been proven ; if bad, it may earn him (as it surely warrants) a longer sentence, but it can never, alone, play any part in his trial, far less convict him.

It was not always so. In England, to this day, the recollection of Judge Jeffreys, and of his reign of terror, known as the " Bloody Assize," is still fresh in the public mind, so awful is the legacy of his deeds. H. B. Irving, in his " Life of Judge Jeffreys," is inclined to ' whitewash ' him, but nothing can withstand the evidence of that judge's brutal words and acts, and we have cause to be thankful that such a creature has disappeared for all time.

That was England, but we in our own land have no cause to point the finger of accusation only at our southern neighbour. They may not have made such a noise in the outside world, but we have had more than one of the Judge Jeffreys type sitting in our own courts and pronouncing sentences with a callous disregard for human dealings and public conscience.

To my way of thinking, the most picturesque ruffian who ever donned a judge's wig was Lord Braxfield. Robert Macqueen, as he was named before assuming his title, was a Lanarkshire man, born at Braxfield in 1721, and admitted to the Bar in February, 1744. He entered his chosen profession at a time when the law was overwhelmed with duties. Of course it is well, indeed only fair, to con- sider the civil and legal setting of that date. We are here just a generation removed from the Covenanting times. The Highland clans were armed and lawless. Sheriffmuir was a recent memory ; and the '45 was still to come. The Union with England was even then lamented in more than one quarter, and strong methods alone could control the unruly section of the lowland populace. Those were days when a public execution occupied pretty much the place now usurped by football, with the possible exception that greater numbers of the fair sex, amongst them ladies of the highest caste, flocked to the sport of seeing a fellow-creature turned off a ladder. Some of the sights witnessed in those days are really too horrible for narration, but the stories are available, in contemporary records, for those who desire the proof.

It was, then, into such a setting, not too refined, where human sufferings, to say nothing of human life, were not regarded as we look upon them now, that Robert Macqueen later to be elevated to the position of a judge of his fellow creatures, with power of life and death in his hands, entered upon his career in the law.

When the butchery which followed the '45 was waning, and when even the government had satiated its blood-thirst, there were other and more important national wrongs to be set right. The processes consisted of forcing the holders of antiquated feudal rights to relinquish their claims on the payment of awarded compensation. These were not merely important, they were delicate operations, impinging on vested interests held for many generations by the ruling families. This was work for the best brains in the legal faculty, and here Macqueen found his place and established his name for the manner in which he conducted his briefs.

It was but a step to higher honours. In 1773, under the title of Lord Braxfield, he was called upon to succeed Brown of Coalstoun as a Judge of the Court of Session. Seven years later he succeeded Boswell as Lord of Justiciary; and when, in 1788, Miller of Barskimming was promoted to the Presidency, Braxfield was appointed as his successor to the important position of Lord Justice Clerk.

As we have seen, Braxfield was called to the Bar in 1744; elevated to the Bench in 1773, and as he survived for seventy-eight years—he died in Edinburgh in May, 1799

—he had a fairly long innings. It is the manner in which he comported himself during the public term of his life round which our interest centres.

His name, fading now with the passing of our quickly-accelerating years, made at one time a rather unsavoury tradition. More than one writer has used him as a leading character, and we have but to refer to R. L. Stevenson's unfinished novel, "Weir of Hermiston," to get a glimpse, and that anything but complimentary, of the judge's family life. Stevenson expected this novel to be his master-piece : these are almost his exact words in referring to that work, and the pity is that his sudden death wrote *finis* when the plot was at an acute stage.

Perhaps it would be well to describe this man. The following graphic picture is in the words of Lord Cock-burn :—

"But the giant of the Bench was Braxfield. His very name makes people start yet. Strong built and dark, with rough eyebrows, powerful eyes, threatening lips, and a low growling voice, he was like a formidable blacksmith. His accent and his dialect were exaggerated Scotch ; his language, like his thoughts, short, strong and conclusive . . . With his intellectual force, as applied to the law, his merits, I fear, cease. Illiterate and without any taste for refined enjoyment, strength of understanding, which gave him power without cultivation, only encouraged him to a more contemp-tuous disdain of all natures less coarse than his own. Despising the growing improvement in manners, he shocked the feelings even of an age which, with more of the formality, had far less of the substance of decorum than our own.

"Thousands of his sayings have been preserved

and the staple of them is indecency. . . . . Almost the only story of him I ever heard that had some fun in it without immodesty was when a butler gave up his place because his lordship's wife was always scolding him. ' Lord ! ' he exclaimed, ' Ye've little to complain o' ; ye may be thankfu' ye'r no married to her.' "

There we have the judge's portrait, drawn in strong lines by a master of the art, one who from his own career was a consummate artist at summing up his fellow men, and who judged not alone by appearance, but who could almost read the thoughts as they were taking shape in a lesser mortal's brain. The extract quoted is not by any means full ; indeed the sweeping exposure of Braxfield's brutal nature, of his jests when sending a prisoner to Botany Bay, or to the gallows with an insulting flippancy, are illuminating illustrations of how the law was conducted in the eighteenth century.

When Braxfield was taking a commanding part in the political trials of 1793 and 1794, to quote again Lord Cockburn, " He was the Jeffreys of Scotland." It often happened that there were difficulties in formulating a prosecution, and in such instances Braxfield's rejoinder was : " Let them bring me prisoners and I'll find them law."

On one occasion, just prior to the opening of a jury trial, as one of the jurors, Horner by name, on passing behind the judge's seat to take his place in the jury-box, Braxfield, who knew the man, leant back and in a loud whisper said, " Come awa', maister Horner, come awa', and help us to hang ane o' thae damned scoundrels."

Sometimes, whether of intention to gloat over his victim and see him wince, or simply from subconscious habit, he would voice his thoughts aloud. Once when listening to the protests of innocence on the part of a young prisoner, he muttered in a tone audible throughout the court : " Ye're a verra clever chiel, man : but ye wad be nane the waur o' a hangin'."

When counsel for the prisoner, on another occasion, was about to open his address, Braxfield again showed his thoughts—and ultimate decision—by muttering aloud : " Ye may spare your pains : we've determined tae hang him anyway."

But it was not only the prisoner at the bar who came under the lash of the judge's bitter tongue. Two well-known advocates—remember the times, and the social manners—had spent the previous evening in passing the bottle. Next day their duties called them to plead before Braxfield, and that worthy soon grasped the significance of their condition. Leaning over the bench he said : " Ye may just pack up your papers and gang hame ; the tane o' ye's riftin' punch and the ither belchin' claret and there'll be nae guid got out o' ye the day."

Can one picture such a scene taking place in a court of justice to-day ? But then again, we must remember the times. An illuminating incident of a contemporary judge illustrates that factor better than most. One morning a servant maid was washing out the close in the old High Street when a rather tipsy gentleman, on approaching her, asked to be directed to John Clark's house. Looking up at the enquirer, the maid replied : " But you *are* John Clark ! " " Yes, yes, I know," was the rejoinder, " but it's his house I'm looking for."

There were few abstainers in those days ; and even at a much later date, when the late Professor Blackie was asked to preside at a temperance meeting, he took the chair under a misapprehension of the true purpose of the gathering, but soon clarified his position in his opening remarks.

This is what he said : " I cannot understand why I am asked to be here : I am not a teetotaler—far from it. If a man asks me to dine with him and does not give me a good glass of wine, I say he is neither a Christian nor a gentleman. Germans drink beer, Englishmen drink wine, ladies tea, and fools water." This anecdote is perhaps a little away from our subject, but at least it is illustrative of views which died hard.

Whatever his failings, Braxfield did not lack for physical courage. The years 1793-4 formed a critical period in our history, and it fell to his lordship to sit in trial of such men as Palmer, Muir, Gerrald, Margarot and Skirving. At that time he was Lord Justice-Clerk, and so endowed with considerable responsibility. One historian, far from taking the popular view which earned for our subject the title of " The Hanging Judge," praises him for his firmness in carrying out what he conceived to be his duty. Our authority—I had almost written our apologist—dilates on Braxfield's bold and fearless front " at a time when almost every other person in authority quailed beneath the gathering storm."

That is as may be ; but Thomas Muir, the advocate, Fysshe Palmer, the clergyman, and the other Radical agitators, were all found guilty and sentenced to fourteen years' transportation, and it is claimed that the sentences were " gleefully pronounced " by the judge in finding them guilty of seditious conduct.

Skirving stood up manfully to the judge and accused him of endeavouring to intimidate him ; he was indeed so goaded that he used the words, " It is altogether unavailing for your lordship to menace me, for I have long learned to fear not the face of man."

One amusing incident in the trial of Margarot arose

when that reformer was called into court to stand his trial. Looking at the prisoner, and speaking in the broad Scottish dialect which he invariably affected, Braxfield said to Margarot, " Hae ye ony counsel, man ? " " No," was the reply. " Do ye want tae hae ony appointed ? " was the next question. " No," retorted the accused, " I only want an interpreter to make me understand what your lordship says."

It is not too much to claim that our country was almost in a state of semi-revolution when desperate men, in a cause they assumed to be right, would go almost any length to secure their aims. Braxfield, too, was not a man who minced his words, not merely on the bench but in his social circle, and a favourite expression, which often fell from his lips, was : " They would a' be muckle the better o' being hanged ! " It was no uncommon occurrence for him to sit in court until midnight, and the proof of his courage— considering the atmosphere—lay in the fact that, his duties being completed, he would walk alone and unattended to his home in George Square.

If direct and to the point in his legal work, Braxfield was not less so in other walks of life. After the death of his first wife, his affections were centred upon another lady of his acquaintance, and his method of courting was characteristic of the man. Calling upon her one evening he said : " Lizzie, I am looking out for a wife, and I thought you just the person that would suit me. Let me have your answer, aff or on, the morn, and nae mair aboot it ! " Knowing her man, the answer was duly given, and on an early date the wedding was solemnized. The lady was Miss Elizabeth Ord, daughter of Lord Chief Baron Ord.

There was no family by this second marriage, but by his first wife, a daughter of Sir Andrew Agnew, he had two sons and two daughters. His eldest son inherited the estate of Braxfield; the second joined the army; and of his daughters, one married the heir to a noble Ayrshire family, and the other was wed to a member of a still well-known Highland clan.

Braxfield was bred to the law, for his father, John Macqueen, was a solicitor who ultimately became Sheriff-Substitute for the Upper Ward of Lanarkshire. Nothing was more natural than that Robert, the ultimate Lord Braxfield, as the eldest son, should adopt his father's profession, so after his early years at Lanark Grammar School he was sent to Edinburgh University. From there, on the completion of his studies, he entered the office of a well-known practitioner, Thomas Goldie, and by dint of study and hard work ventured his fortune by becoming an advocate, with the result we have seen. Notwithstanding his brutal manners he must have been endowed with considerable ability to attain the position which he ultimately achieved.

One fact we may be assured upon: we shall never again see his like occupy the exalted position as a judge over his fellow-men so long as this remains a free country. As already mentioned, a study of the man and his manners is a signpost of the far journey Scotland has travelled in her moral and social outlook. To-day Braxfield's like would be unthinkable.